MW00907975

Personal Finance for the
New Physician

Personal Finance for the New Physician

Money Management for
Residency and Beyond

Daniel R. Lefebvre, M.D.

Copyright © 2007 by Daniel R. Lefebvre, M.D.

Edited by Financial Consultant David P. Hungerford

ISBN: Softcover   978-1-4257-9393-7

All rights reserved. No part of this book may be reproduced or transmitted in any
form or by any means, electronic or mechanical, including photocopying, recording,
or by any information storage and retrieval system, without permission in writing
from the copyright owner.

This book was printed in the United States of America.

To order additional copies of this book, contact:
Xlibris Corporation
1-888-795-4274
www.Xlibris.com
Orders@Xlibris.com
41573

Contents

Chapter 1

Learning Personal Finance Strategy out of Necessity

Imagine being a top student. You excelled through high school, went to a great college, and made it through medical school. Now, starting residency in your chosen field, you are overcome by myriad emotions: joy, raw fear, pride, uncertainty, excitement, and a realization that gnaws at the pit of your stomach—you don't have one cent to your name.

None of the above is difficult to imagine, otherwise you wouldn't be reading this book. It seems unfair. You've worked hard, made the right decisions, and essentially traded the youth of your twenties for the title "doctor." Now you are working 80 hours per week (at least) for the equivalent of $10.00 per hour. What's your net worth? It's likely a very large, negative number (a debt-load of $200,000 or more, depending on what medical school you went to and how much financial support you received from your family). Your friends from college who got jobs four years ago are leaps and bounds ahead of you financially (or at least they should be). They have a four-year head start on earnings and four years less of accumulating debt. Your college roommate probably has some money saved away in a retirement account, and may even have a family and a house!

Should you despair? I don't think so. Some of your friends who are not physicians may appear to be in better financial shape than you, but it is doubtful that many of them have a better earning potential than yourself. As a physician you can expect an increase in earnings by a factor of 3 to 10 (depending on your field and location) after residency/fellowship and having practiced for a few years. True, you have enormous student-loan debt, and you have to manage a stable financial life over the ensuing years of your residency. Plus, future physician-earnings may be on the decline. A report by Robert DeGroote, M.D.,

F.A.C.S., in the Aril 2007 issue of the Journal of the American College of Surgeons *Bulletin*, entitled "The Economics of Managed Care Reimbursement: A rationale for nonparticipation", examined payments for many commonly performed surgical procedures. Dr. DeGroote compared these payments among different managed care organizations and Medicare. He also examined historical payments for the same procedures from 1992. The results were sobering. First, while Medicare had historically been on the lower end of the reimbursement scale, Dr. DeGroote found that the managed care reimbursements were currently all lower than the Medicare reimbursements. Further, Medicare reimbursements for the year 2002 were approximately the same, and oftentimes *less than,* the Medicare reimbursements for the evaluated procedures in 1992! In other words, not only have physician payments not kept pace with inflation, they've actually *decreased* over time in absolute-dollars! Not many people would continue to work at a job for which they hadn't received a pay raise in over 10 years; how many people would continue to work at a job for which their pay was actually *decreased* over the course of time? And speaking of working at a job without a raise, Dr. DeGroote's article reprinted a table from a paper that appeared in *AMA News* (Kazel R. CEO compensation: Accomplishments translate into healthy paychecks *AMA News* May 26, 2003). This table listed the estimated hourly wages of physicians in various specialties as well as the hourly wage of various non-physicians. Of note, Internal Medicine made $51.38 per hour; General Surgery made $83.74 per hour; a weekend RN made $50.00 per hour (about the same as an internal medicine physician!); and managed care CEOs *averaged* $1,423 per hour! That is not a misprint. Managed care CEOs *averaged* one-thousand four hundred twenty-three dollars *per hour!* In my view, this is unacceptable. The way to combat this is to a) become informed regarding physician reimbursement and managed care (which will be discussed in more detail in chapter 8) and b) make the proper personal finance decisions now, early on, so that you can optimally position yourself financially while developing sound monetary habits. By securing your personal finances you will be protecting yourself from potential damages inflicted upon you in the future as a result of declining reimbursements.

And there are more problems than just declining physician reimbursement that need to be anticipated. The number of uninsured people in the United States continues to increase. Risk, in terms of physician liability and litigation, continues to run unchecked as a result of lacking tort reform. Practice overhead continues to rise. The list goes on. But these are not reasons to be overcome by feelings of discouragement. These are reasons to motivate you into learning as much as you can about making proper financial decisions now so that you can live well, treat your patients as innocent people in need of your help and not as adversaries, and to ensure the safety of you and your family's financial future.

I experienced first-hand what the unexpected health issue combined with sub-optimal financial planning can do. A major health problem is definitely sufficient to seriously injure a family's finances. In fact, a study by David Himmelstein of Harvard University documented that one-half of all bankruptcies in the United States result from illness and/or injury, making health care costs the leading cause of bankruptcy (Himmelstein DU, et al. Illness and injury as contributors to bankruptcy. *Health Aff.* 2005 Jan-Jun; Suppl Web Exclusives: W5-63-W5-73). While I was a sophomore at Boston University my own parents suffered financially as a result of health problems. To realize my dream of becoming a surgeon I would have to become financially independent at the age of nineteen.

I found a job working for a truck-parts retailer in Boston. In the mornings, I labored in a warehouse packing old, greasy truck parts into crates in order to be shipped back to the manufacturer for rebuilding. In the afternoons, I drove a truck around Boston delivering truck-parts. The job paid $8.00 an hour; there was no sick-time or vacation-time, and no health insurance. The work was hard and physical, wearing holes through my work-gloves on a weekly basis. I worked 40 to 50 hours per week, and took my classes at BU during the evenings from 6:00 PM to 9:30 PM. Looking back, it was the best period of my life.

In no other time did I develop more quickly than when I worked hard to support myself and pay for my education. I worked alongside men who—probably not making much more money than I was—were raising families. I had enormous respect for them. I vowed never to forget them as I moved on in life. While physician incomes may not be what they used to be, we will still make far more money than the vast majority of our patients. Do not insult people around you (e.g. nurses, clerks, etc.) with complaints about income. Rather, be thankful that you are able to work as a physician. You are one of the few who are able to simultaneously earn an impressive paycheck while truly helping other people. It is a privilege that is worth protecting with sound financial planning.

In order to survive during college I had to become financially savvy. Initially I just did the best I could. With my strengthened determination, my grades at BU actually improved compared to what they had been prior to this difficult time. I received a scholarship that greatly defrayed the cost of tuition. For this I am immensely grateful. I also eventually found work as a medical assistant for a podiatrist. The pay was a bit better, and the job was obviously more appropriate in terms of serving as a precursor to entering the field of medicine. In addition to a better paycheck, and the education that I was obtaining at BU, I was educated in successful medical-practice management. The podiatrist's practice was extraordinarily successful, since he was the go-to podiatrist for Harvard University, the Boston Celtics, and the Boston Bruins. I learned that the key to both business and personal success is: a) be among the best at what you do; b) keep an efficient office staff, with employees who are capable of carrying out broad job-duties; c) keep a neat and professional appearance of your office, your staff, and yourself; d) treat your patients in a courteous manner that will support their recommending you to their friends and family; and e) pay yourself first.

It was the first time that I had heard the phrase "pay yourself first." I don't think that I even fully understood what it meant at the time (you may also not understand it; not to worry—this book will explain it to you). And, unfortunately, as I was about to enter medical school and thus not have an income, it would be a while before I could put the concept into practice. But I knew that it must be the key to successful personal finance—and it is. The concept will be discussed in more detail in chapters 5 and 6.

Over the years, I proceeded to read every personal finance book that I could get my hands on. I learned about different investment strategies. I rid myself of credit card debt and cultivated a very high FICO (Fair Isaac Corporation) credit score. And once I started earning a paycheck as a surgery intern, I had developed a pathway that I believe is the key to coming out of residency in solid financial shape, with a plan that will put me on the right track for growing my finances once I finish ophthalmology training and become an eye surgeon.

I would not be where I am today without the great help of others. From the owner of the truck-parts store, to the podiatrist, to the university scholarship committee, to the support of my friends and family, I owe many people a debt of gratitude. In my view, the best way to honor the help given to me is to offer help to others. Personal finance is not taught in any explicit fashion during high school, college, or medical school. It should be. This book is my attempt to begin the process of filling this educational gap; it is meant to be a brief review of many important personal finance topics presented in a form that you can easily carry in the pocket of your white coat. I look forward to helping you learn to manage your finances as a young physician in a way that is both easy and sound, and that will help to ensure a future for you that is bright and secure.

Chapter 2

The transition: student to resident

So far in my life I have yet to experience a transition that is as abrupt and severe as going to bed one evening as someone who recently finished the fourth year of medical school and waking up the next morning as a surgical intern in a very busy urban hospital. Probably like most medical students, the second half of my fourth year was very relaxed and pleasant. I got married (to someone who was also a fourth year medical student) during that time, and we spent part of April on our honeymoon in Italy. What a great place! What a great time! But the honeymoon was about to end—internship was about to begin. If you are currently a medical student nearing this transition-point in your life, then this chapter is for you.

Unless you matched to your home institution, you will likely be moving to a new city or town. Nobody likes moving, but at least in this situation you should have time on your side (since most graduations occur in May and internship orientation generally begins during the last week of June). If you can, try to move into your new place a bit before orientation begins (later in the book we'll examine the pros and cons of renting versus buying a place). Moving early will give you an opportunity to adjust to your new place, develop a routine, learn your way around your new neighborhood (especially becoming familiar with how to get to and from the hospital; you don't want to figure this out for the first time at 5:00 AM), and you will have time to begin setting up your finances so that once your training starts, much of your finances will be on autopilot. Your time will be limited during the next few years, and having a solid and automatic financial plan will be key to ensuring that you stay on course and begin the process of establishing wealth.

Of course, your time won't be completely monopolized by your job. With the 80-hour work week, you will be in the hospital for less total hours than your colleagues who trained before this regulation was implemented. But you will be tired. Less total hours worked per week per resident equals less total number of residents in the hospital at any given time. This situation is worsened by many community hospitals closing, causing academic centers to be fuller than ever while attempting to accommodate this patient-shift. The result: you will WORK 80 hours per week. The same, if not more, amount of work still needs to be accomplished in a given week. This work will be accomplished by fewer people in the hospital, so your work-density has effectively increased as a consequence of spending less time in-house. When you are out of the hospital, you are going to want to unwind and enjoy yourself. But shouldn't you be saving money and not going out and spending your money? Isn't that the whole point of this book?

Not exactly. The point of this book is to educate you about wise financial decisions. This includes a) being frugal, b) paying yourself first, c) placing your money in the appropriate locations so that you can find the optimal balance between safety and growth, d) saving money in the long run (by achieving and maintaining a great credit score, paying less interest on loans, minimizing purchase depreciation), and e) generally simplifying your money management by putting it on autopilot. Direct-deposit of your salary, internet banking, and internet investment management make it easier than ever to pay your bills and save your money with minimal effort. And you will still be able to have some fun, I promise. Relaxing when you are not in the hospital is, in my opinion, a great allocation of resources. It just needs to be done in a balanced manner. Think of how much easier it will be to maintain this balance when you have your finances in order, on automatic pilot, instead of just "winging" it.

Speaking of allocating resources, what is the pre-intern supposed to do before that first paycheck? How can you allocate when you don't have any resources?

Well, unless you are receiving significant financial support from someone else, the time between medical school and internship can be tricky: there is a definite cash-flow problem. The world of financial aid seems to ignore this dilemma, since student loans only allow for a period during which you are matriculated at that school (i.e. until the day of graduation). You are not explicitly covered for getting a moving van, eating, and paying your security deposit and the first month's rent of your new place. If you anticipate that this period is going to be a problem for you, DO NOT plan to float through it by living on a credit card. Instead, you should consider a private "residency relocation" loan.

These loans go by different names, but they are the cleanest way to obtain funding to cover your moving and living expenses while you wait for your first paycheck to process. I recommend applying for such a loan through the same provider that handles your medical school loans. In this way, you will be doing business with a single company (i.e. simplifying things) and this will be with a business that is endorsed by your medical school (i.e. the financial aid office). My loans were handled by SallieMae (*www.salliemae.com*). I obtained a private residency relocation loan from SallieMae called the MedEx loan. The online application was easy, and the approval process was quite speedy. The funds were transferred into my checking account via direct deposit. The interest rate was 9% and there was a two-year grace period (i.e. no payments required for two years—although you won't want to sit on this for two years because, during that time, interest will be compounding on the debt). I had the money available in time to sign the lease on my apartment with the required security deposit and first month's rent, plus enough to cover renting a moving truck and living expenses until early July.

Finances aside, many people have different theories on how to mentally prepare for internship. I was scared, and I read various 'Surgery On-Call' books cover to cover—I'm not sure that it helped very much because it's very difficult to retain this sort of clinical information simply through power-reading. Again, balance is the key; it's probably better to relax and do some light reading than to view this as a time to cram for an exam. Before you know it, you'll be hearing the alarm buzzing at 4AM for your first day of internship—you'll want to be tan, rested, and ready.

Internship was an amazing experience. On your first day of internship you may be thinking: "I don't deserve to be called 'doctor.' What do I know?" On your last day of internship, while knowing that you are not yet an expert in anything, you will feel confident as a clinician. You *will* feel deserving of the title "doctor," and rightly so. I hope that by applying the ideas set forth in this book, you will release your mind from worrying about your money, enabling you to concentrate more time and energy into developing as a physician and thus arriving at the above realization earlier than you would expect.

Chapter 3

Student Loans

According to the American Medical Association, almost 90% of medical school graduates have outstanding educational debt, with 72% of medical graduates owing at least $100,000 (the average educational debt was $130,500 for the medical school class of 2006). These figures include both undergraduate and medical school debt, but not non-educational debt. Over 40% of graduates have significant non-educational debt (such as credit card debt) averaging $16,689.

It is a testament to the calling of medicine that so many people are willing to take on this enormous debt-load in order to become physicians. The argument associated with whether forcing future doctors to assume such debt (compared to medical students in other nations in which medical education is highly subsidized, if not free) is an interesting debate, but it is not the topic of this book. Learning how to deal with this debt is.

Stafford Loans

There are various flavors of educational loans. Those who are or were enrolled at American institutions of higher education are no doubt familiar with Stafford loans, which are government-guaranteed student loans named in honor of the late Senator Robert T. Stafford of Vermont. Stafford loans generally have an interest rate that is lower than privately obtained educational loans. For example, as of June 2007, Stafford loans are charging approximately 6.8% interest. On the other hand, recent reports have shown some private student loan interest rates exceeding 13%! This is possible since private student loans are essentially unregulated, a problem that New York State Attorney General

Andrew Cuomo is currently looking into since, with rising tuition costs, more students are needing to borrow private educational loans in addition to their already maxed out federal student loans. With such large debt burdens, high interest rates can really affect the finances of students over the long-term.

Interest accrual on a Stafford loan is affected by whether the loan is subsidized or unsubsidized. A subsidized Stafford loan has its interest paid by the government while the student is matriculated and for up to three years of post-graduate training (such as residency). This type of loan is awarded based on financial need. According to studentaid.ed.gov, the maximum amount of subsidized funds available to a medical (i.e. graduate) student is $8,500 per year. Once this limit is reached, money is borrowed from the unsubsidized pot, which allows you to borrow an additional $10,000 per year (for 2007) on top of your subsidized loans. Unsubsidized loans are not awarded according to financial need. The total cumulative Stafford loan debt (subsidized plus unsubsidized) is currently $138,500 for graduate students.

For unsubsidized Stafford loans, interest begins accumulating as soon as the loan money is disbursed. As the interest accumulates it will be capitalized (usually every quarter, i.e. three months), which means the interest owed gets added to the principal balance. As time goes on, the total amount owed increases in an accelerated fashion. You've heard of "compound interest," and this is one of the beauties of investing and saving—it's the key reason why one should begin saving early. Well, the same mechanism that allows savings or investments to grow over time via compound interest is the very mechanism that can greatly add to the amount you owe for a loan that has had its interest capitalized.

Let's say that you have $100,000 in unsubsidized debt at 7% interest. After one year in non-payment, the total amount owed would be $107,000. Assuming you are still in residency and you go another year without making payments, you would then owe $114,490. The reason the amount is not an even $114,000 is because the interest that accrued over the previous year ($7,000) was added to the principal balance. During the next year interest was charged not on the original amount of your debt ($100,000) but instead on the new, capitalized balance ($107,000). During the third year, if you didn't make any payments, your debt would grow to $122,504.30! It's easy (and painful) to see how this debt could get out of hand very quickly. For this reason, interest owed should be paid when possible to avoid interest capitalization.

There's one more benefit of Stafford loans that deserves mentioning. A Stafford loan is forgiven in the event of your death. This is important because it means that if you were to die prematurely, your spouse or dependents would not become liable for your Stafford loan debt. A dreary thought, but something to know about nonetheless.

Private Educational Loans

If your borrowing needs exceed the funds available to you from Stafford loans, you will need to venture into private educational loans. These often have less-desirable interest rates than Stafford loans, as previously described. Also, private loans are usually not forgiven in the case of your death (whereas Stafford loans *are*). If you code, your spouse or co-signer for the private loan *will* get stuck with the bill if this is stipulated in the private loan promissory note—so read the fine print.

Still, private educational loans are a much-preferred method of funding rather than trying to cover living expenses, etc. on a credit card. At the time of writing, the national average interest rate for a standard credit card according to bankrate.com is 14.8%. Some credit cards have interest rates as high as 29.9%, which in most states is considered usury (i.e. "loan-sharking"). The reason many credit card companies are based in Delaware or North Dakota is because these states have not limited usury interest rates in a successful effort to attract credit card business headquarters. You should definitely be able to find a private educational loan with better terms. You will also have a grace period with an educational loan (i.e. an extended time during which payments are not required). You will not likely find a similar deal with a credit card.

In all cases, I hope that you were able to make it through medical school while assuming the least amount of debt possible. Frugal living as a student will pay off in the form of thousands of dollars of savings in interest paid over the repayment of your student loans. If you went to a less-expensive medical school, congratulations—this will translate into major savings over the long-term life of your student loans.

Loan Consolidation

Assuming that you are reading this as an about-to-graduate student or as a resident, the damage is already done. You can't un-borrow money, so it's time to optimize your student loans. First, label a folder "Student Loans" and keep all paperwork there. Even though much correspondence is conducted via the internet now, you should keep some hardcopies of your loan information. You need to know exactly how much you owe and to whom.

One of the benefits of consolidating your student loans is simplification. You will end up with one or two big loans (one each for the subsidized and unsubsidized funds). This will make it much easier to get control of your loans, both logistically and psychologically, through being able to concentrate on a single payment with a single fixed interest rate.

The interest rate for a consolidation loan is determined by the weighted average of the interest rates for all of your outstanding loans. That is, the interest rate of a specific loan is given strength in the average according to the loan balance to which it applies. There are online calculators that can help you determine what your interest rate might be with a consolidation. Check out *https://loanconsolidation.ed.gov* to see what your potential savings could be.

A consolidation loan may actually not save you money over the long-term since its interest rate is simply based on your current loans' interest rates. Some lenders, such as Sallie Mae, offer a "best rate" guarantee, in which they calculate your consolidated loan interest rate based on the best rates that were available to you over the course of the current academic year. Even if this doesn't lead to lower overall costs, a consolidation loan still might allow you to use your money to greater advantage by enabling lower monthly payments. Your original loans may have a more limited selection of repayment plans, whereas a consolidation loan can offer a variety of extended payment terms. If your interest rate is very low (such as equal to or less than the rate of inflation), it will benefit you to lower your monthly loan payments and instead contribute more money towards your retirement investing account.

To be eligible to consolidate your loans they must be in the grace period, repayment, deferment, or forbearance, and you must not have an outstanding application for another loan. Since the grace period is the time immediately after graduating during which no payments are required, you do not want to truncate your grace period prematurely. Some lenders, such as SallieMae, will hold your consolidation disbursement until just before your grace period expires, thus allowing you to realize the maximum grace period benefit.

Loan consolidations can be either federal or private. Your eligibility depends on the composition of your original loans. This is a complicated topic that is subject to subtle changes with time, so the best advice is to sort out the details with your financial aid advisor and your loan company. An important difference is that a federal consolidation loan should still forgive the loan debt in the event of your death. A private consolidation loan may not.

There are many lenders that offer loan consolidation services. The advice I received, and the advice I will give, is to stick with the lender from whom you obtained the majority of your medical school loans. You likely came into contact with your lender through your school's financial aid office. This means that your school felt comfortable recommending this lender to you. In business and finance, there is something to be said for a referral or an endorsement. If you choose to shop around for a new lender, most schools have a preferred lender list; you can use this to help guide you. Indeed, there is currently controversy regarding preferred lender lists and institutions of higher education, which was ignited by New York State Attorney General Andrew Cuomo's investigations regarding school-loan lending practices. Still, at least a preferred lender list indicates a working relationship between your school and a lender, which is better than blindly responding to loan consolidation junk mail, with which I'm sure your mailbox is no doubt overflowing.

Regardless of whether you stand to realize savings or better repayment terms from consolidating, it's still worth it simply to have all of your loans handled by a single lender. It will certainly be easier to keep track of one bill instead of many, and as a new physician, time saved is priceless.

Repayment: management and postponement

If you borrowed a residency relocation loan to pay for your moving expenses and cover you until your first paycheck arrives, you will want to pay this off as quickly as possible (within one to two years maximum), since such a loan may carry an interest rate upwards of 9%. One option is to transfer this balance to a credit card with 0% interest for balance-transfers for 12 months. This is a specific case in which a credit card can be a valuable financial tool—*if* used appropriately. You MUST pay the balance off within the allotted 12 months. Should you not pay the balance off within this time period, the interest rate will convert to the standard interest rate listed in your terms of agreement, which can in some cases be over 20%. Often these balance transfer deals require an initial transfer fee of about 3% of the balance. This still may be worth it. Another option is to take advantage of a term offered by the American Express Blue Card, currently 4.99% interest (with no transfer fee) for the life of the balance. Again, your goal should be to pay this balance off within one to two years maximum. While doing this, do not use the card to carry any other balances such as purchases, etc. Once you begin earning a paycheck, you should never make a purchase "on the card" and not pay the balance in full that month. "Plastic" can be a good tool for simplifying finances (such as buying groceries, gas, etc.) in that it will help you track your spending, you may be able to earn rewards or cash back, receive warranty extensions, etc., all with having the benefit of a single monthly bill to pay. But you must pay that single monthly bill every month *in full, always, without exception.*

Regarding the repayment status of your student loans, there are a variety of ways to deal with these while in residency.

Immediately upon graduating your loans will begin their grace period. For Stafford loans, the grace period lasts six months, during which time no payments are due. And while subsidized Stafford loans will not accrue interest, unsubsidized Stafford loans will continue to accrue interest (as they have been doing since the moment the money was disbursed).

After the grace period, you will enter repayment. There are various repayment schedules among lenders that affect your monthly payment amounts at various time-periods throughout the course of repayment. These need to be investigated on an individual basis. Generally, you should concentrate on reducing debt that has higher interest rates (e.g. credit cards, residency relocation loans, etc) first; if your consolidated student loan has an interest rate of 3%, marry it! Pay the minimum on a 3% loan and use remaining funds to eliminate high-interest debt and to invest in your retirement savings.

By extending your payments over a longer period of time, a consolidation loan can reduce the amount of your monthly payments. This does, of course, increase the total amount of money that you will pay for the loan in total. But if your interest rate is very low, you may want to extend the repayment of your educational loans / consolidation as long as possible in order to make better use of your money now. That is, it is better to invest money in a low-fee index mutual fund (more about this in chapters 5 and 6) that you can expect to earn 9 or 10% over the long-term than using that money to pay-down a loan that charges only 3% interest. This option becomes even more lucrative when you factor in potential interest rate reductions for a good payment history. My consolidation loan through Sallie Mae offers a 1% interest rate reduction after 48 on-time payments. That means after four years of making payments the interest charged for my loan would be 2%! And it may be possible to lower this even further; signing up for automatic electronic bill-pay may lower the interest rate an additional 0.25%, bringing the interest rate down to 1.75%. This is *almost* free money, and, if you can get your interest rate down to a level like this, you should not be in a hurry to pay off your student loan.

But during the initial years of training you may find that the monthly payments required for your loans are unaffordable, even with the extended payment plans (and your minimum required payments may well be out of reach if you have substantial debt and live in a city with very expensive rent). You may need to postpone repayment of your loans altogether. There are two classifications of loan postponement while in residency: deferment and forbearance.

Deferment should be the first option for postponing payments. With deferment, subsidized Stafford loans still continue to have their interest covered by the federal government (although, as previously stated, the unsubsidized loans will continue accruing interest that you can—and should—elect to pay each quarter in order to prevent interest capitalization). There are different classifications of deferment; hopefully, you won't qualify for the 'unemployment deferment,' but if you are unmatched, this option is there for you. For most others, loans can be postponed via 'internship' deferment. While in residency, you will likely be eligible for the 'economic hardship' deferment. This eligibility is determined by comparing your income to your estimated monthly loan payments. If you've maintained or consolidated your loans with a reputable lender with a good customer-service record, initiating deferment should be a relatively painless process. The customer-service representative will be able to direct you to obtaining the correct deferment option, determining your eligibility, and completing the process. Usually the economic hardship deferment option is assigned one year at a time, so you will have to reapply annually.

If you are not eligible for deferment and you still need to postpone your student loan payments, you can apply for forbearance. Forbearance is a less-desirable way to postpone payments because, unlike deferment, during forbearance the federal government will not cover the interest payments on your subsidized Stafford loans. In forbearance you will receive a quarterly statement detailing the interest that has accrued over the past three months on both the unsubsidized *and* subsidized loan balances. You have the option to pay this; again, doing so will prevent the interest accrued from being added to your principle balance so that you avoid paying interest on interest in the future, thus lowering the total loan cost over the life of the loan. Forbearance also has as an option the ability to pay a monthly loan payment that is less than what you would be required to pay through the standard repayment plans. This may be a good option for you if the interest rate on your loans is, for example, greater than the rate of inflation (which is currently about 3 to 4% annually). By doing this, you will prevent your principal balance from outpacing inflation, thus saving you money over the life of your loan(s).

Depending on your specific financial circumstances (amount of debt, salary in your particular city, loan interest rates, rent, etc.) you may not want to postpone loan payments. Your lender will offer different repayment plans, some of which may be interest-only for an initial period that, over time, has an increasing monthly payment amount. Some plans use a more 'standard' approach with a fixed monthly payment over the whole repayment period (which may be as long as 30 years). Changing these factors affects the total amount that you will repay over the life of the loan. Obviously, the more extended plans will free up more capital for you each month at the expense of costing more over the long term (assuming that you adhere to the payment schedule).

One option is to use an extended repayment schedule during your initial years of earning (i.e. residency and the early years after training) when your salary isn't so high and then, once the salary goes up, begin prepaying your loans. Essentially all reputable lenders do not charge a prepayment penalty. That is, if your monthly loan bill is $600.00 but you send a payment for $1000.00 (specifying that the added money is to be applied to your principal balance) you will not be charged an added fee. Doing this can save a significant amount of money over the life of your loan. This technique can also be used to your great advantage when paying the mortgage for a home. Prepaying, or biweekly payments, on a 30-year mortgage can significantly reduce the total cost to you over the life of the loan. This is most appropriate if you weren't able to lock-in an extremely low interest rate. If your rate is low (e.g. 3%, which is lower than inflation and well-below expected long-term stock market returns) you probably should not pre-pay your student loans; instead, you should direct your money into eliminating other high-interest-rate debt (such as credit cards) and contributing to your retirement investing account.

Determining which type of repayment schedule to select (e.g. whether to postpone payments, make interest-only payments, or pre-paying) is not completely straightforward. Factors that affect the decision include the total amount of your loans and, most importantly, the interest rates of those loans. A high interest rate (7% or greater) could benefit from pre-paying. On the other hand, the lower your interest rate, the more you should be willing to extend the payments over time. Remember, if you have a student loan with an interest rate such as 2.7%, there is no need to rush to pay this off. That interest rate is less than inflation and well below what can be expected from long-term broad market investments; it's better to direct your available funds towards paying off higher interest debt (e.g. a mortgage or credit card) and investing the money for your future. To summarize: low interest rate → extend payments and use money for eliminating consumer debt and for investing; high interest rate → more aggressive repayment.

Now that we've addressed getting a handle on your educational debt, it's time to look at where you should hang your white coat at night (and I'm not referring to the call room).

Chapter 4

Housing

Your home should be a place of respite that you are happy to return to after a long day of doctoring—this is undeniable. Whether this place should be yours (i.e. you own it) or someone else's (i.e. you rent it) is a different matter.

Credit Report

Prior to setting out to find a place to live, you should make sure that your credit report is accurate. If you haven't done so already, check your credit reports online. I use CreditSecure, through American Express, to keep track of my credit reports (all three) and my FICO credit scores (which basically grade your creditworthiness—ideally >720, which is considered 'excellent' and will get you the lowest interest rates on loans, etc.). Make sure that there are no errors on your reports prior to submitting a rental application. If you do find an error (such as an account that doesn't belong to you) you will have to initiate the process of error resolution. This can be done by submitting the request online at the particular credit bureau's website or via mailing a certified letter to the credit bureau's error resolution department. You will need to include your name, date of birth, social security number, the name and account number of the erroneous account, and a brief explanation of why you believe this to be an error. The Fair Credit Reporting Act requires that the bureaus investigate your complaint and fix the situation as is appropriate. If the item is found to not be an error, it will remain on your report; if it is found to be a mistake, it should be removed. Unfortunately, this is not usually a smooth process. I had an erroneous account removed from my Equifax report only to find that two months later the account had reappeared! I had to get an attorney involved, and even then it took some legal arm-twisting to get the appropriate outcome and have the account permanently removed. Credit report accuracy is not something that is policed except by you, so this is totally in your hands. Your credit reports are worth checking from time to time so that errors are caught early before they inflict any financial harm to you. Plus, it should go without saying that you should pay all of your bills on time since late payments hit your credit rating pretty hard. If you are responsible with making payments on time, have demonstrated creditworthiness by maintaining an account (e.g. a credit card) with a good portion of its credit still available (i.e. the card has >50% available credit), and you've checked to make sure your credit reports don't contain any errors, you should be in pretty good shape.

Renting

Let's start with renting, since it's the easiest and most common arrangement. The first question is: where should you live? The best way to get information about this is to ask current residents at your program. They've gone through this procedure already and should be able to give you good advice. There may be a building that is particularly popular with residents, usually near the hospital and priced within reason. Having a number of residents living there, especially for more than one year, is a great sign.

Different people have different ideas about how close they want their residence to be to the hospital. During internship, closer is better. In the later years of training, it's a tradeoff between convenience and your sense of "awayness." This is, obviously, a personal decision.

Regardless of whether you choose to live very close to the hospital or a good distance away, there are some general factors to pay attention to. If the city in which you are training has public transportation, note how close the apartment is to a train or bus stop. Will you be driving? If so, what is the parking situation like? Apartment buildings may offer parking, but if this is in the center of a city this can get quite expensive; it may be more economical to park your car in a garage a couple of blocks away from your apartment building. Some cities offer residence parking permits that allow you to park on the street—but you have to get lucky to find a spot, and it may be a healthy walk away from where you live. And don't forget where you parked! If you do need to commute to the hospital from your apartment, will it be via car, train, bus, or by foot? How long will this commute take (and how will this be affected by traffic, weekend train schedules, etc)? Do you have a pet? Do you want a pet? Not all buildings allow pets, so check this out beforehand. For most buildings that do allow pets, there are often restrictions (e.g. cats only), and almost always an added fee such as a higher deposit and an extra $50 to $100 per month. If you happen to have a dog, make sure that you will have access to a dog-walking area that you find acceptable (think about night-safety, trash receptacles, etc.). Finally, look for amenities. Does this apartment offer laundry facilities on-site, or even within your unit? Garbage disposal? Dishwasher? Air-conditioning, pool, fitness room? Snow removal? How will you be charged for electricity and water?

Speaking of cost, what is an appropriate amount of rent to pay in relation to your income? Most experts recommend not spending more than 30% of your gross monthly income (i.e. the amount of money you make *before* taxes) on rent. For example, if your annual salary is $40,000 you could allot about $1000.00/month for rent. But this should be viewed as a maximum acceptable amount. Less is better, because it will free up money for other uses, such as paying off debt, investing, and having some fun. Unfortunately, some of the major cities can push this recommended rent to the limit (and certainly even exceed it). Generally, living outside of the city center is cheaper than living in the middle of downtown. Still, some will no doubt have to exceed the 30% maximum because of where they are training. Just do the best that you can to find a good place that balances being nice with not being outrageously expensive. You may have to find some other ways to save money through thrift.

When looking to keep the price down, be careful if you are using the services of a leasing agent. While a leasing agent can be a source of information, and it's nice to drive around town in a car while seeing a bunch of places in an afternoon, always keep one thing in mind: leasing agents are paid according to the rent of the apartment they lease to you. The leasing agent's fee can be a full month's rent, and in some bigger cities even up to two month's rent, so it is in the agent's own interest to rent you a place that is more expensive.

Once you have decided on a place, it's time to submit your application. You will list your occupation, prior residences, and possibly some references. The application process will also involve a review of your credit report. A good leasing agent should waive the typical $35 fee to obtain your credit report. Once the application is approved, you will be offered the lease to sign. Make sure that you read through the lease and that it is agreeable to you. Yes, there is a lot of verbiage, but it's worth the extra ten minutes to ensure that you agree with what you are signing. The most important thing to check is the rent! Make sure that the figure you were quoted is the same figure that appears on the lease. Also, check for other relevant clauses such as pet fees, maintenance fees, utilities, etc.

With signing the lease comes paying your deposit. Most often, you will need to pay one month's rent as a security deposit and the first month's rent. Some places will also charge the last month's rent in addition to the above charges, for a grand total of 3-months rent. This can be a sizable check, so plan ahead. As we've discussed, paying for this as you're leaving medical school and waiting for your internship paycheck to arrive can be tricky, and this is a prime example of why a residency relocation loan may be necessary if you don't have a significant savings account or the ability to borrow this money from family.

The good thing here is that this money isn't just disappearing into thin air. You will be paying for your first month of rent (and maybe the last month's too). The security deposit should be returned to you as long as you don't live like a barbarian and destroy your apartment.

The security deposit should be held in an escrow account. This means that the money is held in an account that is separate from the general business account of the landlord. Funds will hopefully earn interest while in escrow—this interest is yours. It may be paid on a semiannual basis or upon return of the security deposit to you. Do not put yourself in jeopardy of losing the security deposit. When you first move in to your new apartment, make a close examination of the unit. Look for any damage (walls, doors, appliances). Make sure the carpeting / floors are in good condition. Make sure that the bathroom is acceptable to you. If you find anything that is sub-par, take a photograph of it and make sure that you bring this to the attention of the landlord. It should be well-documented if it is something that isn't going to be repaired (such as a carpet stain).

When it comes time to move on, allow for extra time to clean the apartment. Clean the stove and refrigerator. Make sure there is no mildew in the shower. Vacuum the carpeting and try to fluff up any areas where furniture might have left an indentation in the carpeting. While packing, you will no doubt fill many trash bags with crap that you've accumulated over your stay. Do not forget to discard these garbage bags! Leaving garbage bags in your apartment for the maintenance people to throw out is sure way to be charged a fee out of your security deposit. Fill in nail-holes on the wall from where wall-hangings were placed—you can buy wall plaster packaged for this very purpose from any hardware store. To really be safe, try to walk through the apartment with your landlord once you are finally ready to leave. This will avoid any surprises. By following these tips, you should get your security deposit back without any problems.

Another cost to consider is renter's insurance. Many places will require this; even if it is not a requirement at your building, it is still a good thing to have. Renter's insurance covers damage that you might cause to the property. For example, if you let the bathtub overflow and cause damage to the floor you will be liable for the expense of the repair—this is where renter's insurance can be handy. Renter's insurance also covers personal injury lawsuits that someone could bring against you for an injury they suffered while in your apartment. Finally, renter's insurance can offer protection in the event of property theft. When setting up a policy, make sure that you incorporate theft coverage for the cost of *replacement*, not actual cash value. You will also be able to set the amount of your deductible. The deductible is the amount of money that would come from your pocket before the insurance would pay. For example, a $500.00 deductible means that if your laptop was stolen and the cost to replace it is $2000.00, you'd pay $500.00 and the insurance company would pay the remaining $1500.00.

In most large buildings with a security desk, the likelihood of being the victim of theft is quite low. For the most part, renting can be a comfortable experience, and for many (if not most) residents, it is the wisest choice. While a renter, you have the ability to make a phone call and have your heater fixed; you don't need to worry about the roof leaking (and the associated costs of having to fix or replace it); as a renter, you don't have to mow the lawn, rake the leaves, shovel the snow, or worry about anything other than keeping the inside of your space tidy. When your time is limited, this can be a great benefit. Sure, you won't be building any real estate equity while renting, but it is a safe way to live. Over the long term, to accumulate wealth you ought to be a property owner, not a renter. But in the short term (<4-5 years), you could actually lose money as a homeowner.

Buying

You may have heard others comment on how it only makes sense to consider buying a house if you plan to live there for at least five years. The reason for this is that when you buy a house, much of the money that you spend during the first few years really doesn't buy you equity in the home. For many, the entire first year's monthly payments are applied to interest only. The principal (i.e. the non-interest debt on the home) remains unchanged. The equity is your portion of the principal that you have paid off (in addition to any appreciation, i.e. increase in value, the house may have acquired). Add to this bank fees, attorney fees, and the down payment, and you can see how it will take a few years to recover these costs and start making some financial headway. When considering real estate as an investment, realize that, over the long term, housing prices will tend to follow the rate of inflation. However, over the short term, housing prices can be extremely discordant with inflation—the value of a home can be extremely volatile, which is why at some times a person may rake in the dough from buying and selling a house, while a year later someone may barely break even on such a move.

In fact, the issue may not just be about breaking even. If you purchase a home and plan to live there for a shorter period of time (< 5 years), you run the risk of losing money. Let's say that you've been making payments for a few years and you have started to reduce the principal balance. You can't assume at this point that if you could sell the house for the same price that you bought it for you would break even. A realtor, on average, charges a 6% commission from the sale price. Worse, your house might have depreciated (i.e. lost value) as a result of changes in the housing market. As of the writing of this book, this is a definite possibility. If your house is worth less when you're selling it than when you bought it to the point that the selling price is less than the principal balance that you owe against the house, you will have to come up with the difference.

That is, to sell the house, you will have to *pay* money out of pocket to close your mortgage because the money earned from its sale will be insufficient.

On the other hand, some may see buying as a smart choice either because of the particular market that they are in and/or they plan to be there for 5+ years. For these people, there are certainly potential benefits. For one, there can be a significant tax incentive. All paid interest on a mortgage is tax-deductible. That means you can subtract the interest that you pay from your gross earnings—this will in turn reduce your taxable income and subsequently lead to a lower tax bill. Second, there is the potential to make money when you move, assuming you've been able to accrue equity in the property, either through principal reduction or property value appreciation (hopefully both).

Of course, we've all heard the saying "it takes money to make money." This may be particularly true with purchasing a home. And the first thing on everyone's mind at this point is the down payment.

The down payment is an amount of money that you pay to the bank upfront in order to reduce the total amount of money that you will be financing. It also indicates that you've been able to save a significant amount of money, which the bank in turn views as an indicator that you'll be able to make regular mortgage payments. In most cases, the down payment is somewhere between 10 to 20% of the total cost of the property. Usually a larger down payment translates into a lower interest rate, which can mean a lower monthly payment and a lower total cost over the life of the loan. Of course, it's essentially impossible to save up, as an example, $20,000 while you are accumulating debt as a medical student. And forget the residency relocation loan—a down payment on a house can't be made from another bank loan. If you don't have the option of having a family member or friend assist you with the down payment, there are still options available to you.

Equity sharing may be an option for getting help with a down payment. With equity sharing, a second party (e.g. a relative, an investor, etc.) covers the down payment and writes this expense off as a tax deduction by categorizing your house as a business property. You and the contributor of the down payment become co-owners of the property. As collateral for this venture, the second party holds a second mortgage or deed of trust to the property. This means the second party has the option of selling the property to recoup expenses if you default on the loan. As you can imagine, this could get awkward if you were in this agreement with a friend or family member and the deal went sour. Ideally, you would refinance the property in less than 5 years (assuming that you were able to build equity in the property and/or that the property appreciated significantly in value). Refinancing would enable you to buy-out the second party, thus making you the sole owner of the property.

Some loans offer "100% financing," which means the entire cost of the house is financed (i.e. no down payment required). These are often targeted especially to young physicians. Some loans will even offer greater than 100% financing—these loans will finance an amount greater than the purchase price of the house, which can cover fees and moving expenses, etc. Sometimes the interest rate isn't as good, although if you have an excellent credit score (>720) you ought to get a preferred rate. The key is to shop around and check the online web-forums (such as studentdoctor.net) to see what kind of terms other residents are getting.

Along with a low or no-deposit mortgage comes PMI: private mortgage insurance. This is literally an insurance policy on your mortgage that covers the lender in the event that you default (i.e. stop making payments) on the loan. The PMI may cost a few hundred dollars per month, depending on your total mortgage, income, credit rating, etc. In some cases, the entire first year's PMI premium (payments) will be due in full at the initiation of the mortgage. This amount would still be less than a conventional down payment, so it can be a workable option. Even better is having the PMI premium paid by the lender in exchange for a slightly increased APR (annual percentage rate). Over the short term this option is very acceptable, if not preferable, because the premium is in a way free. Remember, during the first year or so, practically all of your mortgage payments will go towards interest on the loan—and these payments are tax deductible (up to $1 million, which shouldn't be a problem for you). If you sell the house in a few years it will be as if you had free PMI. If you end up staying in the house, you could refinance and get a better interest rate. Regardless, you can (and should) cancel PMI once you've amassed at least 20% equity in the home.

Let's back up and discuss the new term Annual Percentage Rate (APR). You may have seen this on credit cards, private loans, etc. Isn't it just another way of referring to the interest rate of a loan? Well, almost. The interest rate is, obviously, the interest that is charged on a loan over the course of one year. But lenders don't just rely on interest alone to make money. There are often other fees that can be associated with a loan, such as initial start-up fees, account maintenance fees, PMI, etc. Further, lenders may differ on how they compound the interest for a loan (daily, monthly, semi-annually, etc.). In these cases, different lenders could report the same "interest rate," but end up charging you more or less money in actual repayment. The APR attempts to account for these differences so that the borrower has something to compare lenders by. It's as if the interest rate is your GPA and the APR is your USMLE score. So when comparing lenders make sure you put more emphasis on APR than just the advertised interest rate.

The key in looking for a mortgage is to shop around. With the ease of conducting business over the internet, you should have no problem investigating the different terms offered by various lending companies. There are a variety of lenders who specialize in "doctor loans." Regarding these, it's helpful if you know someone who has used a particular lender who can recommend them. The web-forum studentdoctor.net has a finance message board where people will often post what kind of terms they're being offered, as well as recounting personal experiences with customer service, etc. This is a great way to get an overview of what rates are being offered at the particular time when you are researching the loan process.

Let's talk about a mortgage. What exactly does it mean? People use the term all of the time, yet many people are unable to precisely define it. The word may originate from Old French, meaning "death vow," so it's a fairly serious agreement! A mortgage is literally a contract that specifies the terms of a loan used to buy property. The property serves as security for the loan. This contract specifies that if you (the borrower) do not hold up your end of the contract (i.e. make payments) the lender will foreclose the property. Foreclosure is when the lender takes the property from you and sells it in order to recuperate the cost of the loan.

One factor that may affect one's ability to make monthly payments as agreed upon is the specific type of mortgage. The two broad categories of mortgages are fixed-rate and adjustable-rate mortgages (ARM).

With a fixed rate mortgage you get exactly what it says: a fixed interest rate. You will know precisely what your monthly payments will be over the life of the loan at the expense of (possibly) a slightly higher interest rate. These mortgages can be obtained for 10, 15, 20, and 30 year terms. A 30-year mortgage will grant you smaller monthly payments (because the total cost of the house is spread out over more time). Of course, the total amount that would be paid over the life of the loan with a 30-year term will be substantially more than with a 15-year term.

Adjustable rate mortgages are probably better for a resident who plans to have the property for the short term. The reason for this is that ARMs generally start out with a "teaser rate." This is an exceptionally low interest rate that is offered for the first year of the loan; it can be as much as 3% below the standard interest rate. An exceptionally low interest rate is good because it will allow you to generate equity in the property more quickly. After this first year, though, the rate will adjust to follow the assigned index of the loan.

Most ARMs follow Treasury Bill interest rates. Treasury Bills, or T-bills, are one of many vehicles that the federal government issues to finance its own debt. A bond is nothing more than a contracted loan with a purchase price and a maturity value; a bill is a type of bond that matures relatively quickly (months instead of years). Essentially, the buyer of a T-bill is a lender of money to the United States government. The T-bill is auctioned on a Friday for a certain discounted price. The price of T-bills and other Treasury securities is determined by many complex factors, including the state of the economy, general supply and demand for low-risk investments such as bonds, and the actions of the Federal Reserve Bank. In one, three, or six months, when the bill matures, the purchaser of the bill will be paid the maturity face value of the bond. The percentage difference between purchase price and maturity price is the index from which banks will base their ARM interest rates. How often a bank adjusts your interest rate, and by how many points above the T-bill index it aims to keep your interest rate (i.e. the "margin"), are the terms that you must understand in your ARM.

So while you can expect the interest rate of your ARM to increase after the first year, you will be offered some protection by what is called a "cap." Caps limit the magnitude by which your interest rate can change within a year's time. Take as an example a 2% per year cap. If your teaser interest rate is 3%, regardless of how high the bank interest rates go within a year, the maximum interest that you could be charged during the following year is 5%. Of course, the rate could increase another 2% during the next year if the index continued to rise. Your protection here is the lifetime cap, which limits by how much your interest rate can increase in total—for example, not more than a 6% increase over the life of the loan. In other words, starting with a 3% "teaser rate," your interest rate should never exceed 9% at any time during the life of the loan. This is an important figure to take note of when planning your future. When agreeing to an ARM, you should be aware of the maximum expected monthly payment (i.e. what would your monthly payment be if the loan reached its maximum interest rate). This should not be a figure that causes you to go into cardiac arrest. That is to say, your initial payments in an ARM should be viewed as temporary, and the possibility that the maximum expected payment could become your actual payment should be anticipated. This way, you can avoid getting into serious financial trouble down the line if the T-bill index continues to push your rate up. It's like flying an airplane. Good pilots anticipate an engine failure during takeoff—that way, if the engine ever did fail, the pilot would be prepared to take appropriate action. With an ARM, you should anticipate the maximum expected payment so that you can handle it if it ever becomes your actual monthly payment.

While caps put a limit on how high your interest rate can go, some lenders decided to put caps on how *low* your interest rate can go. Such a limit is called a "floor," and it is best avoided. When the economy causes interest rates to go down, you want to be able to benefit maximally. This is yet another reason why it is so important to shop around for a mortgage. You want a "no floor" ARM.

As we've seen, interest rates will change, and this will affect your monthly payment and the total amount that you will pay for a loan. Beware of a potential problem: it is possible to get into a situation in which your interest rate has increased but the bank has kept your monthly payment the same. In this situation, depending on the discrepancy between the new interest rate and the amount of your monthly payments, you may be starting to sink *further* into debt as opposed to paying off debt. If your monthly payment is less than the amount of interest your loan accrues in a month, then your loan will begin *growing* even while you are making payments. This is bad, because the unpaid interest will be added to the principal balance (capitalized). This will accelerate interest charges, and put you further behind. The ominous name for this downward spiral is "negative amortization."

Strange term. Let's break it down. "Negative." Okay, that sounds bad. "Amortization." Well, that has "mort" in it, which I think means death (e.g. mortician, mortuary, mortal, etc.). That's right. Amortization means "to deaden" in Latin. In financial terms, amortization describes the paying down of a debt through installments of payment. Negative amortization is the enlargement of debt while making payments on that debt. Remember, debt is something that you want to kill. Allowing it to grow while making payments is bad. The way to avoid this is to make sure that your monthly payments change accordingly when your interest rate changes.

So we've presented fixed-rate and adjustable-rate mortgages as the two main categories of real estate loans. As you probably expected, it's not that simple. There are many different sub-types of ARMs.

A hybrid ARM is exactly what it sounds like. It is a mixture of two types, part fixed-rate and part adjustable-rate. With a hybrid ARM, the loan starts out as a fixed-rate mortgage. After a period of time, the loan switches, or "resets," to an adjustable rate mortgage, in which the interest rate changes (floats) according to the index and margin that were laid out in the terms of the loan. A 3/1 hybrid is a fixed-rate mortgage for 3 years, and then resets to an adjustable-rate mortgage with interest adjustments at 1-year intervals. Fundamentally, a hybrid ARM shifts some of the risk associated with interest-rate uncertainty from the lender to the borrower. In exchange, the lender may offer the borrower better terms.

An option ARM (also known as a "pay-option loan") allows the borrower to choose which type of payment schedule is followed for a given month. The borrower may pay according to a 15-year fixed, 30-year fixed, interest-only, or some other specified minimum payment. Obviously, this carries with it the opportunity for negative amortization, so it is not an optimal loan-type. Its allure is mostly to those whose income can be highly variable. A seasonal employee may have such a loan, making higher payments during times of higher income, and then switching to alternative minimum payments during times of low income. Obviously, you are not in this situation as a resident, and you should not really consider an option ARM too seriously.

Finally, you may have heard of "balloon payment" mortgages. These are infrequently used in residential real estate. Briefly, you may have a short-term mortgage (such as 7 years) during which time you make monthly payments at a 30-year rate. Obviously, this discrepancy is insufficient to cover the total cost of the loan. At the end of the term, a large final payment is due to cover this difference. This is known as the balloon payment, and it can be devastating if one is not financially able to pay it.

The discussion of mortgages and interest rates would be incomplete without addressing "points." To obtain a better interest rate, a lender may require you to pay an upfront fee. One point is simply 1% of the total loan amount. Thus, one point on a $200,000 loan would be $2,000. If you plan to be in the property for the short term (5-10 years) paying points is not worth it. Remember, mortgage interest is tax deductible, so it is better to have a slightly higher interest rate (the payments for which you can deduct from your gross annual income at tax time) in order to avoid paying hard cash upfront at loan initiation.

Now that you are educated about the different types of mortgages, it's time to go find a house, right? Not so fast. One thing you can do to make yourself a more appealing (and eventually successful) buyer is to become pre-approved for a loan. This literally means that you have applied for a mortgage through a lender, the lender has examined your application and credit report, and has ultimately approved you for up to a certain amount of money. Make sure that your pre-approval has a "lock-in" agreement, which locks in the terms under which you applied. Without the lock-in, it may be possible for the final terms to change once it comes time to actually purchase the house. And make sure that the terms do not include a prepayment penalty. If you make payments greater than the scheduled payments, or you sell the house, you don't want to be charged extra fees.

Getting these details straightened out during the pre-approval process will put your mind at ease, since you will know that you've qualified for financing with good terms. But more than this, it can give you an advantage in a sellers' market, in which competition for properties is keen and houses sell quickly. If you see a house that you like, you will make an offer. If you are not pre-approved, the seller will have to wait while your application is reviewed. To the seller, this wait may be unacceptable if there are other potential buyers who have their financing already established. By having pre-approval, sellers may take your offer more seriously, and you will be able to move quickly in a competitive market.

So, with pre-approval under your belt, it's now time to search for a house. There are many ways to do this and many points to consider. First, you should decide how much you want to spend. This figure should not necessarily equal the maximum that you were pre-approved for, but should be an amount that will allow you to live comfortably while being able to save and invest in your future in addition to paying off any consumer debt that you might have.

In terms of total debt, lenders like to see it eat up less than 36% of your gross monthly income. Some lenders will exclude student loans from this calculation. Even if they do, you shouldn't. The goal here is not to get the best mansion you can possibly get approved for. Your goal is to get a house and to be smart about it. It is important that you have funds available for retirement investing, utilities, etc., and yes, having fun. If you opt for a zero-down-payment mortgage, your debt should occupy an even lower percentage of your gross monthly income.

For the actual monthly mortgage payment, tradition has been to not exceed 28% of your gross monthly income. This figure gets adjusted upwards somewhat in markets in which housing prices are extremely high (New York, Los Angeles, San Francisco, etc.). This is not because it is good for you financially, but simply because almost no one would be able to purchase a house in these markets otherwise. For a couple that makes $80,000 per year, a monthly mortgage payment of $1,900 would be acceptable (28% of gross income). Today, this would translate into an approximately $250,000 property. If this couple could find a house that they liked for less money, that would be better.

Obviously, there are many factors that can affect the price of a house. We've all heard the phrase "location, location, location!" On a macro-scale, this is true (e.g. Orange County, CA compared to Ward County, ND). It is also true at the micro-scale (suburbs, neighborhoods, school districts, at the end of a street versus at an intersection etc.) You will pay more for a better location, but it might be a smart move. People will always want to live in nice areas, with good schools, and tolerable commutes. When it comes time to sell the house, you will benefit by having bought in a good location.

A realtor can help you with this search. Again, being driven around and shown houses is a nice way to spend an afternoon. Just remember that realtors work on commission, so you need to take responsibility for yourself—don't be pushed into a house that is more expensive than you should realistically buy.

Some sellers, in an effort to not lose 6% of their selling price to the realtor, have begun to list their houses privately. The website ForSaleByOwner.com lists houses that owners are selling privately, without the services of a realtor. You may be able to find a great deal through such an avenue. Just make sure you have an attorney assist you in the final proceedings. Without the realtor, you will want someone with professional merit on your side to ensure the deal is legally safe and sound.

And don't even think about buying a foreclosed house, or trying to pick up a great deal on a "fixer-upper" in an attempt to "flip" the house like you've seen on TV. The insane market that allowed so many novices to make fast money is pretty much over. Plus, these properties involve headaches that you do not want while you're a resident. It's best to skip this altogether.

Okay. You're pre-approved. You've found the house that you like, and it fits your budget. Now it's time to make the offer. Your offer to the seller is a legally binding commitment to buy. It sometimes includes "earnest money," which may be $1,000 to show your good faith. If you weren't pre-approved, you will want to have a "mortgage contingency clause" in the offer, which states that if you are not able to get approved for the loan the offer is void and your deposit will be refunded. Often, the offer may be below the asking price in hopes that the seller accepts it. In markets that are "hot," offers may be *above* the asking price, with the hopes of beating out other buyers. Once the offer is made it is reviewed by the seller. The seller can reject it, issue a counteroffer to you, or accept your offer.

If the offer is accepted, congratulations! The bank will have the house appraised to make sure that the house is worth the money that is being lent to you. The house is almost yours. Now comes the closing. You will need to have proof of homeowner's insurance. Do not give in to the combination life/disability/unemployment insurance that may be offered to you by your lender, which makes the lender the beneficiary. If you are going to pay for insurance, you want your spouse or whoever you wish to designate to be the beneficiary, not the bank.

At the closing you will also need a certified check to cover the closing costs, which can include lender's fees, attorney fees, taxes (sale, state, local property), and deed transfer fees. These can total up to 5% of the loan amount, so you really need to plan ahead for this. It may be possible to roll the closing costs into the loan in exchange for a slightly higher interest rate. Again, this can be good because the interest will be deducted from your federal tax liability. You will inspect the home, sign the papers, and hand over the check. The house is yours.

Now that you own the house, you own the mailbox. And in the mailbox there will be bills from your lender. It is time to begin paying these according to the terms of your loan, avoiding negative amortization as we've discussed. In fact, you may be tempted to pay more than what is due. This is a great way to build equity quickly and reduce the total cost to you over the life of the loan. One of the most popular and least-painful ways of doing this is to pay the mortgage biweekly instead of monthly. That is, instead of paying your mortgage every month, you pay half the payment every two weeks. There are services that will set this up for you, and it definitely saves money over the life of the loan. The reason is because you get in an extra full month's worth of payments in every year. Prepaying reduces your principal faster, and thus it reduces the amount of interest that you are charged.

Prepaying may not be the best idea for everyone, though. First of all, if you have any credit card debt you must devote yourself to eliminating it first. You can think of paying bills as investing, with the rate of return equal to the interest rate on the debt. Is it better to invest money at 20% return or at 6% return? Obviously, it's better to invest for a guaranteed 20% return, which is essentially the return you would realize by paying off a credit card with a 20% interest rate. Similarly, over the long term, your investment accounts should be returning ~10% per year (as has been the history of the stock market as a whole over many decades). If you are not already contributing the maximum to your retirement accounts, you should not be prepaying your mortgage.

Condominiums

A few words about condominiums: these can be attractive, especially to first-time buyers, because they are generally less-expensive than traditional stand-alone houses and there is less maintenance required from the owner. Often, there are amenities such as a swimming pool, a workout room, a lobby, and nice landscaping. Further, the owner doesn't need to worry about cleaning the pool, mowing the lawn, etc. This is taken care of by the management of the property, for which the owners pay monthly fees.

For all of these good aspects of condominiums, there are some drawbacks. First, on average, a condominium experiences less appreciation within a given market compared to a comparable house. Furthermore, should the market deteriorate, a condominium can lose value much more quickly than a house. For these reasons, it can be difficult to build equity. If you plan to live there for a short period (less than 5 years), it is quite possible that the property could be devalued at the particular time during which you plan to sell it, thus creating the potential to lose real money.

And since you own a part of a larger whole, there is generally less freedom associated with condominium ownership. You can paint the walls in your dining room, but you can't paint the exterior of your unit whatever color you want to. There also may be limitations on pets or even children.

Risk is also different in a condominium. In a house, you are in charge of your own finances. With a condominium, if some of the other owners default on their payments, the difference will need to be made up by the other owners.

Finally, do not make the mistake of equating living in a condominium to living in an apartment. With an apartment, if the roof needs to be replaced, that's not your problem. For a condominium owner, replacing the roof can be a very big deal. Basically, the cost of the repair gets divided among all of the owners within the property. So if you move from an apartment and purchase a condominium, the days of carefree living are over.

In some areas, a condominium may be the only chance at property ownership that a resident may have. Around the major cities, housing prices can be so expensive that co-op ownership is the only viable real estate option available to young professionals. In this case, take the following recommendations into consideration:

- The best co-op option is a townhouse. You will have a better chance of resale when it comes time for you to move.
- Purchase a two-bedroom unit. This will also have a better resale value than a one-bedroom, or worse, a studio.
- Buy a unit in a place that is mostly owner-occupied. Owners living in a co-op is a great sign. It means the people who own the units don't mind

living there. And, most importantly, the owners will treat the area with greater respect than renters.

- When you examine the property, it should be in excellent condition. The last thing you want to do is buy a townhouse and then two months later get hit with your portion of the bill for completely re-landscaping the property!

- Meet the board of directors. Make sure that they seem smart and that they have cash reserves for non-paying property owners. There will always be some members who will default on their loan or not pay the monthly maintenance fees. A smart board accounts for this, and this planning will soften the financial impact of such events.

*   *   *

This has been a long chapter. It's a complicated topic. The goal of the chapter was to educate you about some of the intricacies of renting and home ownership. For most residents, renting will be the way to go. For those who decide to buy, hopefully this chapter has informed you about the major points that you will need to know about for the major life-event of home-ownership. Still, you shouldn't go out on your own and buy a house. When the time comes, it will be important to have someone with experience who you can trust help you through the process. Even though you've read about how to put in a subclavian central venous catheter, you still want someone looking over your shoulder the first time you attempt it. Buying a house should be no different.

Chapter 5

Physician—Pay Thyself (first)

Nothing is more important than paying yourself first.
Nothing is more important than paying yourself first.
Nothing is more important than paying yourself first.

They say that people remember something that is repeated to them three times. I hope this is true, because the best thing that you can do to create a sound financial future for yourself is to begin saving regularly in a retirement account.

As a resident, you are working hard for your money. At 80 hours per week, you're making about $10.00 per hour. And this can be stressful, exhausting work. Yet, for all of your efforts, you likely approach your finances in the following way: Your paycheck arrives every two weeks, hopefully via direct deposit into your checking account. You pay your rent, cable television, parking, buy groceries, take out some cash for lunch and coffee at the hospital, go out to dinner one or two nights per week, get that new textbook you've had your eye on, etc, etc. Your spending might be limited by the availability of funds in your bank account. Once all of the above expenses have been taken care of, you take the money that's left over and invest it in your future, right? Probably not. In fact, if your hospital offers a 401(k) or a 403(b) plan, you probably didn't sign up for it, because, after all, you're "only going to be there for a few years." Plus, you're too young to worry about saving for your future. And you have student loans and other consumer debt. Shouldn't you eliminate all of this debt first before saving for your retirement?

[like a slow-motion horror movie scene] Noooooooooo! The above line of thinking is *entirely* backwards. It is true that when approaching debt you should prioritize according to the interest rates that you are being charged. This does not mean that if you have debt you should prioritize in a way that has you only

paying off that debt at the expense of investing nothing. Doing so would cause you to lose the most precious of allies in accumulating wealth: time.

The next two chapters are the most important chapters of this entire book. If this book accomplishes nothing other than teaching you how to pay yourself first to start saving *immediately* for your future, it will have been, in my opinion, an enormous success.

Many self-help finance books address the issue of paying yourself first. You've probably heard this expression on television, the radio, or read about it in magazines. What does it mean exactly? Your paycheck arrives in your name; doesn't that mean you are already getting paid first? Not really. A better way to view your paycheck is as a preliminary transfer of funds from your employer into a purgatory-for-money, i.e. the checking account. A checking account does not pay interest (at least nothing substantial enough on which to comment); it is merely a transfer station from point A to point B for money. So, money showing up in your account every two weeks is not the equivalent of having paid yourself first. Paying yourself first means taking a portion of your earnings (such as 10% of your gross salary) and contributing it to your retirement investment account. This should be the very first "bill" that gets paid before you even consider paying rent! It should become a way of life so that it doesn't even require you to think about it once you've established a mechanism for doing this. Ideally, the whole process should be on autopilot.

401(k) / 403(b) / 457

The easiest (and most financially productive) way to automate this process is to participate in a 401(k), 403(b), or 457 program through your hospital, if it's available to you. What are these plans, and why are they named with a combination of numbers and letters? Is this a mathematics problem that involves imaginary numbers? Isn't this supposed to be easy?

In fact, it is easy. 401(k), 403(b), and 457 literally refer to the sections of the United States Internal Revenue Code that describe the tax conditions for these retirement savings plans. A 401(k) is available through a privately owned corporation, while 403(b) and 457 plans are available through a government or non-profit employer. For simplicity, I'll just refer to the 401(k) in the following text—but the information also applies to 403(b) and 457 plans.

In the good old days, people worked for companies that offered pensions. When the worker retired, the pension plan kicked in and offered a salary (usually a percentage of the previous salary based on the worker's position in the company and length of employment), as well as health insurance, etc. As health insurance and other costs have risen, companies have shied away from the pension model in an effort to cut costs. As a result, the burden of retirement funding has been shifted to the worker, and employee-funded retirement accounts have taken over.

With the 401(k), employees contribute a portion of their salary, *before taxes*, into an investment account sponsored by their employer. Often, the employer contributes a certain amount of money to "match" what the employee contributes, up to a certain maximum match that is company-specific. This serves as an incentive to encourage people to contribute, since participation is not mandated and it is all too easy to not participate, thus being left with nothing other than social security benefits upon retirement. Most experts feel that the 401(k) model is superior to a pension plan because 1) it gives the employee some control over their own retirement funds, and 2) the funds are entirely transportable. Compare this to a pension plan. If someone was employed by General Electric (GE) for 15 years and then accepted another job at Lockheed, the 15 years of GE pension eligibility vanish. Starting the new job at Lockheed, the employee is starting from ground zero.

Consider a 401(k) model. An employee has contributed to her 401(k) while working at GE for 15 years. This employee has managed to save a considerable sum. Now, she is to begin working at Lockheed. Does this mean all of the money she has saved is gone forever? Hardly. She can move the funds over to her Lockheed 401(k) and pick up exactly where she left off. This is one of the attractive features of the 401(k). It's why it is entirely okay, and in fact necessary, for you to begin participation in such a plan immediately. Even though you may only be at a particular hospital for a limited time, you should take advantage of pre-tax savings while you are there (and also benefit from employer-matching, if it's available—although the informal survey I conducted by randomly calling hospitals to see how many matched their residents' 401(k) contributions revealed a disappointing number: zero). Upon moving on, you will simply transfer your 401(k) savings to your next stop.

So let's talk about the specifics of a 401(k). As stated, this is an employer-sponsored retirement plan. Money is contributed by the employee on a pre-tax basis, effectively deferring federal income tax on this money until the time of withdrawal in retirement. The money is invested (more on that in the next chapter) and, over time, the money grows. Unlike a non-retirement (i.e. taxable) account, the earnings that your investments create are free from taxation. That is, capital gains (money earned from the sale of appreciated stocks) and dividends (semi-annual payments from stocks) are reinvested in your retirement account and are not subject to taxation.

There are two main types of 401(k) plans. The most common type is called participant-directed. In this model, the employee directs how this money is invested (i.e. chooses which mutual funds, bonds, etc. in which to invest the contributed money). The other type of 401(k) is called trustee-directed, in which the employer has appointed a group of trustees to manage how the employees' contributions are invested.

One of the ways 401(k) plans are so special is that they allow both employee and employer contributions. The employer may *match* a certain portion of what the employee contributes. This may be a fixed amount, a percentage of the employee's contribution, or some form of profit-sharing (i.e. the employer contributes an amount proportional to the performance of the company). Some employers may have a match that is vested, which means the employee must be with the company for a certain time-period before matched funds are available. Nevertheless, employer-matching is possibly the most enticing reason to participate in the 401(k) because it is literally free money.

Unfortunately, as already stated, I haven't come across a hospital that offers a match to resident 401(k) contributions. But don't worry too much. The benefits of pre-tax contributions still make 401(k) participation worth it. In addition to reducing your current taxable income (and therefore reducing your federal income taxes) you actually gain money faster through your investment's earnings because these gains are not eroded by income tax and/or capital gains tax.

Let's take a look at an example of investing using a tax deferred account versus a taxable account. Assume that you have $10,000 of income on which you have yet to pay taxes. Let's also assume that you are in a 30% tax rate on any income that you make. Figure 1 shows the differences in how the monies grow between the two different accounts. The first shows $10,000 of tax-deferred money earning 10% per year over 30 years. The full $10,000 is invested because no taxes are paid on it (hence, tax deferred). After 30 years, that original $10,000 will be worth $158,631.

Now, using the above parameters, let's take the same $10,000 and invest it in a taxable investment vehicle. Note that now you only have $7,000 to invest because you will have to pay 30% (i.e. $3,000) of the original $10,000 towards income taxes. As you can see, after 30 years, the tax-sheltered account has almost $50,000 more value than the taxable account! Why? The extra $3,000 that did not go to pay income tax instead compounded over time and allowed you to earn more money on your investment. Thus, allowing the money to grow in a tax-sheltered environment is a very important component of wealth generation and retirement saving.

There is a unique subtype of 401(k), called the Roth 401(k), in which contributions are made on an after-tax basis and withdrawals are realized in a tax-free manner. Still, with this type of 401(k), as with the standard 401(k), investment earnings grow tax-free.

A few words about the 457 plan. While not offered as commonly as 401(k) or 403(b) plans, there are some specific characteristics that you should be aware of regarding a 457 plan if this is what your hospital offers. A 457 plan works the same way as any other retirement plan in that it is owned by the employer

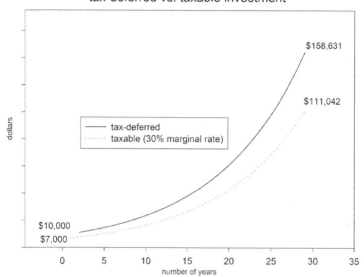

Figure 5.1: Hypothetical result of $10,000 available for investment, either contributed in a tax-deferred manner or on an after tax basis. By contributing to a tax-deferred retirement plan (such as a 401(k)) the entire $10,000 is available for investing. If one had to pay income tax on $10,000, there would only be $7,000 available for investing (assuming a 30% marginal tax rate). Over time, that extra $3,000 of tax deferred money would eventually earn an additional $47,589. [10% annual return;0.21% fee]

and is funded by tax-deferred contributions. Some key differences, however, are that 457 plans do not allow employer contributions (i.e. "matching") nor do 457 plans offer loan provisions—but 457 plans offer the most liberal means by which to withdraw money from your account, as will be discussed in the section on withdrawing funds later in this chapter.

At this point, I hope you are wondering about how to contribute to a retirement plan. That's the easiest part of this whole chapter! You just contact your human resources department and tell them you want to sign up for the 401(k) / 403(b) / 457. They will send you some paperwork, you indicate how you want your contributions made, and that's it! Ideally, you want your contribution made as a percentage of every paycheck. A great starting goal is 10%. The money is taken from your gross pay (i.e. prior to taxation). If you're making $40,000, this would equate to $154.00 per biweekly pay-period. But you can't go wild here. There are limits as to how much can be contributed to a 401(k) in a year. For 2007, that limit is $15,500 over the year. This figure is adjusted in $500.00 increments in response to inflation. If you are over 50, you get an extra allotment of $5,000, for a total possible annual contribution of $20,500. If your employer is matching your contributions, your total annual contribution can't exceed the lesser of your total annual salary or $45,000. As a resident, you probably aren't going to run up against these contribution maximums, but I want you to be aware of them as you consider the contributions that you will be making down the road as a practicing physician.

Now you've gotten interested, and you're regularly contributing to your 401(k). But what happens if the hospital goes bankrupt? Won't you lose all of your money? Thankfully, no. Whereas classical pension plans are not exempt from bankruptcy liability (and thus could be lost in the event your employer went bankrupt), your 401(k) assets are *not* considered liable property in bankruptcy (thus, your money is your money; it can not be taken away in the event of your employer declaring bankruptcy). Just be careful. If you had invested all of your contributions singularly in your employer's or hospital's stock and the company went bankrupt, you could lose your savings. Of course, you should *never* have your money invested in a single asset—that's just absurd. In the next chapter, we'll address how to keep your investments diversified (i.e. spread out in different types of assets) automatically, thus maximizing your long-term growth and minimizing your risk.

Okay, so the hospital hasn't gone bankrupt, but residency is over and you're moving on. How do you keep the money you've invested in the hospital's 401(k) program? That's simple. When you go to a new job, you can easily have your 401(k) assets transferred to the retirement plan at your new employer. There are a couple of ways to move your money. The easiest way to move your nest egg is to have your new retirement plan company perform a transfer. In this instance, the institution that will be receiving the funds simply requests the funds directly from the original holding institution. You do not touch the funds directly and, therefore, this move is not reported to the IRS. The second type of way to move your funds is to perform a true "rollover," in which the distribution of your funds is paid to you in the form of a check. You then have 60 days to make a rollover contribution to your new retirement plan in order for the funds to maintain their retirement-fund status (i.e. tax-sheltered). This procedure will be reported to the IRS, and you can only perform it once every 12 months. If your next employer doesn't offer a 401(k) you can open and transfer your money into an individual retirement account (IRA), which is another type of tax-sheltered retirement investing account.

Individual Retirement Accounts

IRA stands for individual retirement account. Whereas a 401(k), etc. is sponsored by an employer, an IRA is owned and initiated by an employee. In most other respects, though, it is very similar to the 401(k). For example, like a 401(k), funds in an IRA are exempt from bankruptcy liability. Hopefully you won't need to exercise that protection, but it's good to know.

One difference between a 401(k) and an IRA is the maximum amount of money that can be contributed to an IRA annually. An IRA can only be funded with cash, and for the two most common types of IRAs, the annual maximum contribution in 2007 is $4,000 for those less than 50 years of age.

The first type of IRA to discuss is the traditional IRA. With a traditional IRA, contributions are made in a tax-deferred manner. Since the IRA is not administered by your employer, the funds can't be taken from your paycheck prior to taxes. You make the contributions yourself. The good part is that these contributions are then deducted from your adjusted gross income. You therefore reduce your taxable income and, thus, reduce your total tax bill. By doing this, you can again realize the benefits of tax-deferred contributions that were seen with the 401(k). If your salary is $40,000 and you contribute $4,000 to a traditional IRA, your taxable income becomes $36,000 (i.e. 40,000-4,000).

The earnings in your traditional IRA grow tax-free. There are no upper income limits that would prevent you from being able to contribute to a traditional IRA, however there are income restrictions that limit to what degree someone may claim their traditional IRA contributions as tax deductions. For a single person in 2007, the full contribution is tax deductible up to an annual income of $50,000. Above this, the amount of the contribution that is tax deductible phases out to zero when the annual income reaches $60,000. For a married couple filing jointly in 2007, contributions are fully tax deductible up to a combined annual income of $80,000, phasing out to zero by a combined income of $100,000.

The traditional IRA is best for someone who expects to be in a lower tax bracket upon retirement. In other words, someone who is in a 25% tax bracket now can realize immediate tax savings by contributing to a traditional IRA. Then, during retirement, when the person's tax bracket may be lower (e.g. 15%), the withdrawals will be subject to that tax rate (15%), for a savings of 10% over the working-years rate of ~25%. One problem here is that it is impossible to predict what tax rates will be in the future. What we anticipate today as a 15% tax bracket for a retired person could change. In the future, our example retired person might, even with the lower income, be assessed a 25% federal income tax simply because Congress could have increased taxes! So a savings in absolute tax terms is not a guarantee. Nevertheless, many feel that it is worth it to realize a guaranteed tax-savings today. This savings is real, and as a resident, you immediately can benefit from the reduced tax liability.

A great example of this is related to moonlighting. Let's say you moonlight 10 times over the course of a year, making $700.00 (untaxed) for each shift. When it comes time to prepare your income tax return, you will have to claim this $7,000.00 under Schedule C as 'other income.' You will definitely owe tax on this money, and it can change your tax return from a refund to a bill for taxed owed (at 25%, that would be $1750). By contributing to a traditional IRA, you can deduct your contributions from your adjusted gross income. If your total income is less than $50,000, you are eligible to deduct 100% of your contributions. If you contributed $3,000 that year, then you can effectively cut your taxable moonlighting earnings from $7,000 to $4,000, and the tax on that income would change from $1750 to $1,000: there's $750 in your pocket just for contributing to your own retirement account! Another way to look at this would be to think that your $3,000 IRA contribution only cost you $2,250. Either way, this is a real savings that you can realize and appreciate as a resident, when your finances are likely a bit tighter than they will be once out of training.

On the other hand, if your income is greater than $50,000 you will start to lose your tax advantage by contributing to a traditional IRA. By $60,000, you will be completely ineligible for the tax deduction. Reaching this income is quite possible if you are in an expensive city where resident salaries are a bit higher, and/or if you work a lot of moonlighting shifts. In this case, it doesn't make sense to contribute to a traditional IRA because you will pay taxes on your contributions now *and* you will pay taxes on your withdrawals later. This brings us to the *Roth IRA*.

Republican U.S. Senator from Delaware William Roth sponsored the legislation for a new type of IRA that became established in 1998. Known as the Roth IRA, it essentially reversed the model of the traditional IRA. With a Roth IRA, contributions are made with after-tax dollars and all withdrawals upon retirement are *tax-free*. Also, there are less restrictions on withdrawing money prior to retirement. Unlike the traditional IRA, which has essentially the same withdrawal restrictions, penalties, and exceptions as a 401(k), the Roth IRA allows you to withdraw money that you've contributed at any time without penalty (since the contributions were made with after-tax dollars and therefore are not assigned a special status). This is another reason for the popularity of Roth IRAs.

Because of its reversal of the traditional IRA model, a Roth IRA is best-suited for someone who anticipates being in a higher tax bracket upon retirement—the funds are contributed while in the lower tax bracket and then distributed exempt from tax while the person is in the higher tax bracket. For this reason, the Roth IRA is a highly recommended choice for residents who can reasonably assume that their retirement income will be higher than their current income.

Here's another difference between the traditional and Roth IRAs. For a traditional IRA there are no income limits. You could earn $1 million per year and still contribute to a traditional IRA (you just couldn't claim your contribution as a tax deduction). On the other hand, a Roth IRA has income parameters that limit who may contribute. Using 2007 figures, a single person may contribute fully up to an annual income of $99,000; partial contributions after that may be made up to an income of $114,000, after which contributions to a Roth IRA are not allowed. A married couple filing jointly may each contribute fully if their combined income is below $156,000; above this level, partial contributions are allowed up to a total income of $166,000, after which further Roth IRA contributions are not permitted.

There is a way around the income ceiling of the Roth IRA. The federal government has legislated a limitless conversion period in the year 2010. During that year, a person may transfer all of their traditional IRA funds over to a Roth IRA without any income restrictions. The only catch is that the funds will be retroactively assessed federal income tax. Luckily, that tax bill won't have to be paid as one lump sum but can instead be paid over the course of the years 2011 and 2012.

There are some other types of IRAs, including the SEP-IRA (which is for small businesses or self-employed individuals) and the Simple-IRA (which is similar to a 401(k)). These will not be options for residents and are therefore beyond the scope of this book.

So, your hospital doesn't offer a 401(k) and you've decided to go with an IRA (probably a Roth IRA). How do you start this process? Well, great news! Setting up an IRA is actually *easier* than setting up a checking account at your local bank.

First, choose a brokerage firm to handle your IRA. Vanguard (*www.vanguard. com*) is a popular choice because they charge famously low fees (such as 0.21% per year for a Target Retirement Fund). For Vanguard, the initial minimum deposit to start an IRA is $3,000. If you don't have $3,000 ready to go, don't worry. Fidelity (*www.fidelity.com*) as of this writing offers the ability to open an IRA with only $200.00 as long as you sign up for automatic investing (which you really should do anyway). These websites also offer links to help you determine whether a traditional or Roth IRA is best for you. Unfortunately, you aren't going to get a clear-cut answer. Most financial planners seem to prefer Roth IRAs, and given the circumstances of being a physician, it probably is the better choice for a resident.

Once you pick an IRA type, just click through the screens, enter your information, input your bank account information so that you can set up automatic investing, choose an investment (more about this in the next chapter), and you're done. The optimal scenario is to have a fixed amount contributed automatically every month so that you don't have to think about it. And since you are contributing a fixed amount regularly, you will automatically buy more shares when stock prices are low and less shares when stock prices are high—which is exactly what you want to do. This process of automatically investing a fixed dollar amount at regular intervals (e.g. monthly) has been termed *dollar cost averaging.* Over the course of time, through dollar cost averaging, one should end up owning stocks with a lower average cost per stock than if one had randomly bought the stock on a single day when the price was aberrantly elevated. Some have argued that dollar cost averaging is a myth; it may be true that if you had a lump sum (such as $4,000 to fund your IRA for an entire fiscal year at once) you would be better off investing at once, the argument being that by entering the market earlier you can realize a greater return. Since the jury still seems to be out on this, and you may not have $4,000 to invest at once on January 1st of every year, regular monthly contributions that take advantage of dollar cost averaging seems like the best way to go.

The next chapter will detail how to invest your 401(k) or IRA, taking advantage of low-cost index mutual funds, asset allocation, and diversification.

Withdrawing Funds

So let's fast forward. You've had a great career as a physician and you're now retired. There are some rules that govern how you may withdraw your money out of your retirement accounts (either 401(k) or traditional IRA—remember, Roth IRA funds may be withdrawn at any time). Well, the rules first state that you shouldn't be withdrawing until you are 59 ½ years of age. If you withdraw prior to that, you will be penalized an excise tax of 10% on the withdrawn amount (in addition to the standard federal income tax). The 403(b) plan offers more flexibility when accessing your money. The 403(b) plan allows you to take penalty-free withdrawals if you retire at age 55 or later. For example, if you are 57 years old when you retire and you have both a 401(k) and a 403(b) plan, you will have full access to your 403(b) monies, but you will have to wait another two-and-one-half years (age 59 ½) before you can access your 401(k) monies without paying the 10% federal tax penalty. Taking this a step further, the 457 plan is free of any early withdrawal penalty as soon as you are separated from the employer that provided the plan (i.e. you've left that particular hospital) regardless of your age. For example, if you were to retire at age 50 you would have immediate access to your funds in a 457 plan without any federal penalty. As another example, if you're 35 and you finish training and leave the hospital that sponsors your 457 plan, any money you withdraw is free from penalties. Of course, you would still have to pay normal income taxes on all monies withdrawn.

There are circumstances in which you may be able to withdraw funds from your 401(k) or 403(b) plan while you're employed. These exceptions include: withdrawing up to $10,000 for the down payment of your first home; needed money to avoid being evicted or to avoid foreclosure; payment of certain higher education expenses for yourself or your dependents; paying for medical expenses that exceed 7.5% of your adjusted gross income; funeral expenses of your parents/spouse/children; funding certain disaster-related repairs to your primary residence (also known as "hardship withdrawals"). You may also be able to access your retirement funds early by withdrawing them as substantially equal periodic payments (SEPP), which calculates a rate of distribution based on life-expectancy tables. In this situation, once you initiate SEPP, you must continue to withdraw for a period of five years—otherwise, the money withdrawn will be retroactively subjected to federal income tax.

What if you really need the money but don't meet any of the above exceptions? You can borrow money from your 401(k) or 403(b). By taking funds as a loan you avoid the 10% early withdrawal penalty and federal income taxation. The money must be repaid within five years according to the terms and interest rate that are established for the loan. If you happen to default on the loan, the distribution is considered an early withdrawal and is thus assessed the 10% early-withdrawal penalty in addition to federal income taxation.

Whoa! There seem to be a lot of rules here. Is that it? Not quite. There is also an age target by which point you *must* begin to withdraw from your 401(k) / 403(b) / 457 and/or traditional IRA. If you do not begin withdrawing the minimum distribution from your retirement plan by age 70 ½, you will incur a penalty of 50% of the amount that should have been withdrawn (according to life-expectancy tables, etc.). If you are still working at age 70 ½, though, this requirement does not apply.

Don't let all of these rules scare you away from participating in your retirement plan. In a way, these rules are your ally. They make it difficult (but not impossible) to access your retirement money. This is good, because it's bad to withdraw from your retirement savings. Duh! That money is for your future, not for today. And with the money properly invested, you want to keep it in the market, not take it out. Just missing a crucial few days of stock market gains could cost you a fortune in earnings over the long term. Remember, historically, the stock market *has always gone up over the long term*. There have been ups and downs, but, over an extended period of time, it has gone up. Sometimes the market seems to lose value for a relatively long period of time and then makes an astonishing recovery, and it can make remarkable gains within a few short days. If you had taken your money out just before the recovery, only to try to buy back in at the later recovered prices, you would have had an enormous loss of assets. This is a long-winded way of saying it is really in your best interest to not be able to easily withdraw from your retirement funds. But it's good to know that, in an emergency, you could do so.

*   *   *

This chapter may have been a bit confusing, but the summary is simple. If your hospital matches your contributions to a 401(k) or 403(b) then go with that—it's free money! If a match is not offered, consider not participating in your hospital's deferred compensation program and instead set up a Roth IRA. Contribute the maximum that you can since you will likely only be eligible to contribute to a Roth IRA while a resident (i.e. while you still are within the income limitations).

Great. You've taken action and set up your retirement account. You are contributing *automatically* and *regularly*, and your money is invested in . . .

Chapter 6

Physician—Pay Thyself (part deux)

Many people get anxious at the thought of investing. The idea of the stock market and all of the strange terms and behaviors associated with it keep them from really considering what to do with their money. But if you're going to have a retirement account, you're going to be involved with the stock market—and the more you know, the better off you'll be.

This chapter is going to explain a bit about what the stock market is, what some of the terms you may hear on the news or see in the newspapers mean, and how you can use the market to invest your money in a way that aims to find the best balance between comfort and long term gains.

The Stock Market

The stock market is literally a market for trading company stock. That is, companies sell tiny fractions of themselves to investors. The market via which these investors obtain the fractions (i.e. shares) is the stock market; stocks trade from investor to investor (as opposed to from company to investor) in what is known as the aftermarket, or secondary market. The stock market is, in reality, a notion, not a place. The actual trading occurs at places called stock *exchanges*. There is a plurality of stock exchanges in the United States. The largest is the NASDAQ, which is located in Times Square in Manhattan. It trades mostly technological stocks over a completely electronic interface. The second largest stock exchange in the United States is the New York Stock Exchange (NYSE). This is located on Wall Street in Manhattan. The NYSE has trading occur in a face-to-face manner; it's the kind of trading you see in the movies, with people on the floor yelling and making hand signals to each other.

Why does this crazy system exist in the first place? Simple: money. Companies need money to function and to grow. A great way for a company to generate capital (i.e. money) is to sell tiny shares of ownership to investors. The shares are sold at the stock exchange—the company gets money, and the shareholder gets fractional ownership in the company. The company can use this raised capital to promote itself, invest in research and development, etc. If the company's use of the capital is successful, the value of the company goes up, and so does the company's stock value. The company can take its profits and reinvest back into the company (called retained earnings) or it can distribute some of the profits among its shareholders—these are dividends. A shareholder may also sell the stock back to the company or trade it to another investor (in the aftermarket). Profit from a sale is termed a capital gain.

Of course, not all companies are successful. Companies may sell shares to investors, generate capital, and fail. As the company fails, the value of the stock falls. As investors try to unload stock, a couple of things happen. First, the supply of the stock effectively increases, so the competitive price of the stock falls (via a simple supply and demand relationship). Second, other investors view a sell-off as an ominously negative sign, which further diminishes demand for that stock. Nobody wants to buy stock in a sinking ship. So the initial investor who finally sells his shares for a price *lower* than what he bought them for loses money—a capital loss.

With the surge in retirement saving among individuals, participation in the stock market by the general population has become much more commonplace. As a result, retirement accounts have seen an increased rate of return in exchange for assuming increased risk.

It is this fear of risk that keeps many people from taking full advantage of participating in the best stock market in the world. In reality, the market moves along quite well normally. People tend to concentrate on the negatives because that is what gets reported in the nightly news. If the markets have a bad day, it's a major headline. But what is not reported is the correction of the market back to normal, eventually to the point of posting gains. For sure, the stock market can move up and down in an abrupt manner. Uncertainties in the economy, geopolitical events, etc. can all affect the market, sometimes in illogical and frustrating ways. But this effect is in the short term. The market may also trend upwards (a bull market) or downwards (a bear market) over longer periods of time, such as years. But in the long term (decades) the market goes up. Since 1926, the market has lost value in three out of ten years, which means the market has gained value in seven out of ten years. With retirement investing, you are investing for the long term. When the market goes down, you are buying stock that is essentially "on sale." In fact, as a young person saving for retirement, you should *hope* that your early years of investing are during a bear market (i.e. a pessimistic market with declining stock prices). By buying during a bear market you purchase stock at a low price that has "room" to appreciate over the long term. The key to taking advantage of this long term appreciation is to 1) invest at regular intervals, 2) own a variety of securities to spread out your risk (diversification), and 3) *keep your money in the market—don't take it out!*

Let's learn a few more terms so that when events in the stock market are reported in the news, you'll now understand what's being discussed. Perhaps the most familiar line from the news anchor's mouth is "the Dow lost X points today . . ." What is 'the Dow'? It's the Dow Jones Industrial Average, which is an index (list) of the 30 largest publicly held companies. This index was created in 1896 by Charles Dow, founder of The Wall Street Journal. These 30 largest companies are also often referred to as "blue chips," after the most valuable chips used in poker. Blue chips are well-established, large companies that post stable earnings: think General Electric, Coca-Cola, and IBM.

There are many other indices that can be looked at to gauge how the markets are performing. The Dow Jones Wilshire 5000 is an index designed to reflect the entire U.S. stock market (although the U.S. stock market currently has over 7,000 companies represented). The NASDAQ composite is an index of approximately 3,000 technology and growth stocks. The Russell 2000 measures the performance of small companies. One of the most popular of all is the Standard & Poor's 500 (or S&P 500, for short). This measures the performance of the 500 largest U.S. stocks.

One way to refer to the size of a company is by "market capitalization," which is simply a measure of a company's economic size. The figure is arrived at by multiplying the stock price by the total number of shares outstanding (i.e. the number of shares that people own). Large cap stocks are from companies that have values greater than $10 billion, such as blue chips. Mid cap companies have values between $1 billion to $10 billion. Moving down, small caps are valued between $250 million to $1 billion, and micro caps are valued less than $250 million. In very general terms, volatility (the propensity for a stock to gain and lose value) is least for large cap stocks and greatest for micro cap stocks. Another way to look at this is in terms of risk, with large cap stocks having the least perceived risk compared to small or micro cap stocks with the most. Ideally, the tradeoff for higher risk is higher return in the long term.

Stocks can also be classified according to their performance characteristics. Investors who concentrate on "growth" aim to buy stock that they expect will increase in price that could potentially be sold for capital gains. This generally happens when the company reinvests its profits in order to "grow" the business, thus raising its own earnings and, consequently, the stock's perceived worth. Investors may also go after "value" stocks, which are stocks that are seen as underpriced. The goal is to buy these stocks when their purchase price is lower than their calculated worth and then profit when the stocks adjust upwards. "Income" investments are stocks that pay relatively higher dividends. Thus, owning these stocks, the shareholder can receive an "income" through dividend payments. The bottom line is that growth, value, and income can all make you money.

At this point you may be starting to believe that having a bit of apprehension towards the stock market is actually an appropriate emotion! To a point, you are right. What I've presented so far is just the very surface; it gets much more complex, but we don't need to get into too much more detail. You shouldn't be buying individual stocks anyway. What basis do you have to even make decisions regarding stock purchasing? One thing you can bank on, the "hot tips" you see in magazines and on television are not reliable. If someone truly had a great stock tip, would they announce it to the whole country? No way. It's essentially impossible that by the time "new information" finds its way to you, a resident living in the hospital, that there is any real value to it. The market has already accounted for this information through pricing probably way before the person discussing it on TV even learned of it, so stock picking is not for residents since it is a losing battle.

You shouldn't be buying individual stocks anyway because the optimal way to invest your 401(k) or IRA is with mutual funds.

Mutual Funds

A mutual fund is a collective investment that pools the money from many investors into one place and then uses that money to buy various stocks and bonds, etc. (A bond is just a loan to a company—it has a purchase price and a maturity price. The difference between the two is the profit. In general, bonds have less risk and less return than stocks. Bonds tend to go up when stocks are down). The advantage of a mutual fund is that it allows you (an individual investor) to own many different stocks at a cost that is much lower than what it would take to buy each of the stocks individually. Mutual funds also greatly simplify things because you can invest in a whole class of stocks at once.

You buy into a mutual fund; the mutual fund is overseen by the fund manager, who does the actual buying and selling of securities for the fund. Of course, fund managers and their teams don't work for free, so there is a slight cost incurred in owning a mutual fund. This cost is termed the Total Expense Ratio (TER), and it is paid as a percentage of your total holdings (for example 1%). If you hold $10,000 in a mutual fund that has a 1% expense ratio, the fund effectively costs you $100 for that year. There are some additional fees (such as 12b-1, which pays for advertisements, and early redemption fees that penalize you if you take your money out too soon), but the main cost is the expense ratio.

Expense ratios vary among mutual funds. As a general rule, actively managed funds (those with a fund manager who actively buys and sells stocks within the fund according to a specific investment objective with the aim of making a higher profit) cost more than index funds (mutual funds that are not actively managed but simply aim to invest in stocks to mirror a given index, such as the S&P 500). Ironically, index funds appear to outperform actively managed funds over the long term. There are many theories as to why this is the case. Among the most plausible are 1) it's simply impossible to accurately predict the stock market, and doing so puts investors at a disadvantage compared to random or constant stock holdings of as broad a market-representation as possible, and 2) since the actively managed mutual fund has a higher expense ratio, the holders of these funds achieve lowered effective earnings because the fund's gains have been reduced by the higher fees. Plus, an actively managed fund likely has higher turnover with associated trading fees and capital gains taxes. All of this further erodes from actively managed funds' returns. Thus, over decades, actively managed funds on average under-perform (by almost 2% per year) simple index funds like the S&P 500, which simply buy and hold the shares making up the S&P. Despite this, there is no shortage of actively managed mutual funds.

Domestic mutual funds often cost less than mutual funds that are heavily weighted towards international holdings. The reason for this is that it is less expensive for a fund manager to manage a mutual fund in the United States than it is for that same manager to manage a fund that is compromised of companies that are located thousands of miles away.

The main ratings website of the mutual fund world is Morningstar.com. This website has a ton of information and articles related to mutual funds, as well as mutual fund rankings. But just like most rankings systems, it is based on the past—not the future, nor even the present. Do not think that clicking over to Morningstar.com and finding a 5-star fund is the answer to all of your worries. That 5-star ranking is based on past performance. It could be an aberration. In the next year, today's 1-star fund could potentially outperform that 5-star fund. We just don't know.

But there is something that we do know: diversification. Without a doubt, diversification is the key to a stable long-term appreciation of your money. In plain English, diversification is spreading out your investments into different *types* of investments *that are not directly related to each other*. In other words, by putting your money into different investment vehicles (stocks, bonds, money-markets) and into different investment sectors (technology, services, blue chips, emerging markets, etc.) you simultaneously get the maximum return for the least risk; this is the premise of the school of thought known as Modern Portfolio Theory, in which high-level mathematics and statistical analyses aim to find this balance between maximum reward and minimized risk achieved through proper diversification. And investment firms, eager for your business, have made achieving such diversification so easy it's ridiculous.

Often referred to as "life-cycle funds," these mutual funds combine stocks, bonds, cash, and other vehicles such as money-market funds, across different market sectors to automatically keep the fund diversified according to the fund's original investment strategy. The key word here is "automatically."

Over time, as different vehicles and market sectors perform differently, a fund can become unbalanced. As certain stocks die and others have runaway success, the fund would move towards becoming overly invested in the successful component. At first this may seem okay. "Great, I want to be invested in a successful stock." The problem is when the "successful stock" later loses value—you could suffer a major loss. Remember, diversification is the key. So, as the fund moves through time and it starts to become unbalanced, the fund manager sells off some of the stock that has gotten too prominent and uses that earned capital to buy into the other parts of the fund that have become deemphasized. You've heard of "buy low and sell high," right? Well, fund-rebalancing takes stock that was successful and sells it: that's money into the fund's purse from "selling high." Then, the fund buys back into a vehicle that has experienced a low—"buying low." Therefore, this rebalancing act locks in profits by ratcheting capital gains and maintaining the protection of diversification. It's beautiful!

With these life-cycle funds, the way the fund is distributed across stocks and bonds, etc. is related to your age and when you plan to retire. The younger you are, the more volatility (i.e. risk) you can handle in return for higher gains over the long-term, so a younger person should be more heavily invested in stocks. As you near retirement, however, volatility becomes bad—you don't want your money to take a nosedive just prior to leaving the workforce. So as a person nears retirement, the targeted funds shift away from stocks and move towards high-grade bonds, with the goal being stable income generation. Two popular asset allocation funds are the Vanguard Target Retirement and the Fidelity Freedom funds (both of which are "no-load" funds, meaning you don't pay an extra sales-commission fee; you want to only deal with no-load funds). The life-cycle funds are tagged with a year, such as '2040,' which refers to your expected year of retirement. These funds are available in different 5-year increments. As of this writing, the Fidelity fund has an expense ratio of 0.76. Its investment distribution is: 3.6% cash; 83.5% stocks; 11.8% bonds; 1.1% other. The stocks include a variety of different mutual funds, concentrating on domestic growth stocks and moving down to a small but notable investment in foreign securities. The Vanguard fund has an expense ratio of 0.21 (this is what Vanguard is particularly known for—cheap costs). It is invested in: 1.2% cash; 88.5% stocks; 9.9% bonds; and 0.4% other. The stocks of the Vanguard fund are similarly represented by index mutual funds, mostly in domestic growth equities, with some international stocks as well. Part of the way that Vanguard keeps costs down is by investing in its own index funds, and this is what you want.

As stated before, the Fidelity fund has an expense ratio of 0.76 and the Vanguard fund as an expense ratio of 0.21. Recall that earlier I pointed out

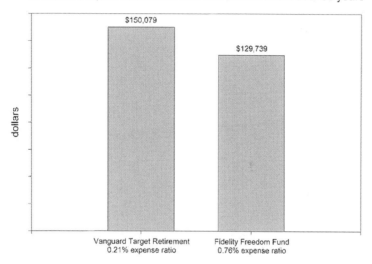

Figure 6.1: Hypothetical one-time $10,000 investment in life-cycle funds demonstrating significance of fund expense ratios. The Vanguard fund generated over $20,000 more than the Fidelity fund over the course of 30 years as a result of its lower expense ratio. A 10% average annual return in a tax-sheltered account was assumed.

how a lower expense ratio can affect your earnings. Here's how. The cost of $10,000 in the Vanguard fund over ten years would be $268. For the Fidelity fund, the cost of $10,000 over ten years would be $978. That's a difference of $710. If we assume an annual return of 10% in the fund, that extra $710 would become $1841 over the next ten years! So by investing $10,000 in a fund with a 0.76 % expense ratio instead of a fund with a 0.21% expense ratio, you will lose over $1800! Now, what would this $710 be after 30 years at a 10% compounded average return? Answer: $12,389. Figure 6.1 illustrates the difference between the two expense ratios after a hypothetical one-time $10,000 investment followed out to 30 years—the Vanguard fund, with its lower expense ratio, beats the Fidelity fund by over $20,000! The message is clear: pay attention to your expenses.

The other message here is the amazing ability of compound interest to create wealth. This ability is inextricably related to time. With compound interest, wealth grows exponentially. The sooner you start, the wealthier you will be. It's as simple as that. What if you could make a one-time investment of $10,000 when you were 18 years old and you retired at age 65; how much money would you have if you earned 10% annually on average in a tax-sheltered account with a fund that charges a 0.21% expense ratio? You'd have $806,215! Almost a millionaire from a one-time investment of $10,000! Now, what if you made that same one-time investment ten years later at age 28? You would then only have $316,828. And what if you waited until after you've been an attending for a few years at age 38? Just $124,507. As you can see, time can be your best friend or your worst enemy, and figure 6.2 shows this in a striking fashion. The person who starts late will need to invest much more money in a relatively short period of time in order to catch up. It's still worth doing, but it's much harder. Therefore, you must start investing as soon as possible in order to reap the benefits afforded by time.

No one is going to make a one-time investment of $10,000 at the age of 18, so let's use a more realistic example. What if you started investing $4,000 per year at age 25 in a life-cycle fund with an expense ratio of 0.21% held in a tax-sheltered account (such as a 401(k) or an IRA). Assuming an average 10% annual return, figure 6.3 shows that by age 65 you would have over $2 million! If this doesn't convince you to get started *today*, I'm afraid nothing will.

It's also important to not ignore inflation. Inflation eats away at your investment returns. The $2 million quoted above will not have the same buying power in the year 2047 as it does today. This is another way of saying it's vitally important to save as much as you can, starting as early as you can, in a tax-sheltered account!

I won't say "get in the game," because it's not a game. It's your life. You've worked hard to become a physician and you deserve a comfortable and well-financed retirement. Start now and make it happen. If your hospital offers

Effect of time on a single $10,000 investment

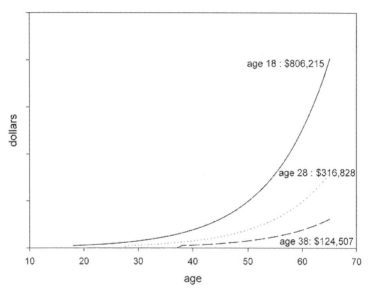

Figure 6.2: The effect of time on investment earnings assuming an average annual return of 10% and a 0.21% expense ratio in a tax-sheltered account. A single $10,000 investment at age 18 generates a value of $806,215. Beginning at age 28 sees this single investment worth less than half: $316,828. Waiting to start investing until the age of 38 sees this one-time investment increase to only $124,507.

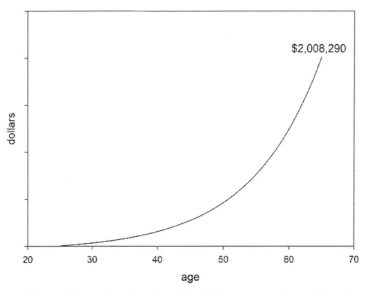

$4,000 invested yearly beginning at age 25

$2,008,290

dollars

age

Figure 6.3: Hypothetical investment of $4,000 annually starting at age 25 and continuted until age 65. Assumes a 10% average annual return in a tax-deferred account with a 0.21% expense ratio.

a match to your contributions within its deferred compensation program (e.g. 401(k) or 403(b)) then sign up to participate with a goal of contributing 10% of your gross salary. If a match to your contributions is not offered, open a Roth IRA instead and contribute 10% of your income automatically every month. Don't even worry about what "the Dow" is doing. In fact, you may want to actively ignore the rants of CNBC's Jim Cramer and the like. Just set up automatic investments in a low-cost life-cycle mutual fund. By doing this you will have taken the most important step of all in planning for an enjoyable future. As your income increases once you are an attending and your contributions exceed the limits of your 401(k) or IRA you can explore ways to diversify your portfolio in a more advanced and tax-efficient manner using individual index mutual funds (some in your tax sheltered accounts and others in regular taxable accounts), the use of tax-managed index mutual funds, and adding some commercial real estate investments to your portfolio via *Real Estate Investment Trusts* (REITs) to hedge against inflation. But, for the time being, contributing regularly to a life-cycle fund should be the foundation on which you begin building long-term wealth for a pleasant retirement.

Chapter 7

Getting from A to B: Your Car

Not every resident will need a car. For example, someone living in Manhattan or Center City Philadelphia can easily survive without a vehicle—in fact, it would be cheaper to *not* have a car. But the majority of residents in the country will need a car. This chapter will give you some information so that you can get from point A to point B without breaking the bank.

You are in an optimal situation if you already have a car from medical school. As long as it is not an old jalopy, you should keep it. Unless you are becoming a pediatric cardiac surgeon, it should last you through the next years of training. Even making the occasional major repair will be more cost-efficient than leasing or buying a car.

If you don't already have a car (or you have one with a grave prognosis), by all means, resist the temptation to "treat yourself" to the lease on a new BMW. Yes, you've worked hard and you do deserve to be good to yourself. At this stage, the best way to be good to yourself is to make smart financial moves that will strengthen your future.

You may have heard the expression "a car is the worst investment you can make." There is some truth to that, and here's why. Let's say you go to the dealership and purchase a brand new vehicle. As soon as you sign the paperwork, get the keys, turn the ignition and drive off the lot, you've just made an investment with a return of *negative* 15% because you paid a "new car price" for a new car. Now you own the car, making it a used car that can only be sold for a "used car price," even though it's a used car with *very* few miles. Bankrate.com reports that a car loses 12-15% of its value per year, and this value can be even higher during the first year of ownership. So if you don't already own a car and you definitely need one for residency, the smartest move economically is to buy a used car.

Pre-owned

Since cars depreciate the most during their first 2 to 3 years of ownership, the best balance between cost and value is to buy a car that is 3 to 4 years old. To demonstrate this, consider the Volkswagen Jetta. A new 2007 Jetta has an average dealer price of $16,490, according to Edmunds.com. This is for the base model, manual transmission, etc. The same model car, only three years older (2004), has an average dealer retail price of $10,706. In three years, the 2004 car likely has ~45,000 miles, any major mechanical flaws should have already announced themselves and been remedied, and the car may even still smell like new inside! But the most important "feature" of this 2004 car is this: a 35% savings.

When selecting a used car, there are a number of points to consider. The most important of these may be predicted reliability. There are a couple of reasons why you should pay attention to the predicted reliability of the used car you are about to purchase. First, you won't be able to depend on new-car warranty coverage. So when buying that used car, you want to minimize the chance of a major mechanical malfunction occurring during your time of ownership. Your used car likely won't be an outright lemon, since that would have been apparent to the first owner of the car and remedied through the dealer. But, after that initial time period, different brands and models of cars are prone to routine equipment failures at differing baseline rates. To reduce your chances of having to make costly repairs in the future, buy a car that is famous for reliability. Consumer Reports (consumerreports.org) annually publishes a collection of car reliability reports. You can check this online and use it to guide you towards a reliable vehicle.

The second reason for selecting a famously reliable car is resale value. If you buy a 4 year old car now and complete 4 years of training, you will come out of residency with an 8 year old automobile. At this point it may be time to sell the vehicle and get another vehicle—maybe a step up in luxury (but still 3 to 4 years old for maximal savings). You will want to sell your 8 year old car outright. Selling a car that is famous for reliability will get you the most potential buyers and you will realize the best recovery of value possible from your car. Nobody wants to buy a 10 year old Dodge Stratus, but the market is full of buyers for a 10 year old Subaru. A quick perusal of eBay as I am writing this reveals a 1997 Subaru Legacy with 150,000 miles selling for $5,000. Meanwhile, a 1997 Dodge Stratus with 127,000 miles is selling for $1,000. This is a great point to remember with *anything* that you buy. Always consider what it might be worth down the line if you sell it in the future. This will steer you towards quality and will pay you back financially when you do end up selling something.

Another point to consider when choosing a car is paint color. Do not buy a car that is bright yellow, or chartreuse, or light purple, etc. Someday you will want to sell the car. You will have many more interested buyers if your car is a standard color (black, silver, dark green, burgundy, navy blue, etc.) than if your car is conspicuously-toned.

Okay, so you've decided on a car model. Consider yourself lucky if you've got the money on-hand to make the purchase, or if you are in the position of receiving the vehicle as a gift for graduating medical school. In this case, you have the greatest hurdle to getting the car already overcome: money. There is a caveat here: if you have money on hand but *also* have high-interest credit card debt, it would be better to pay off the high interest debt and take out a loan for the car—you'll be paying a lower interest rate on a car loan than on a credit card.

If you don't have cash ready-to-go for this purchase, you are going to need financing. Used car financing generally charges a couple of percentage points more than new car financing, but the money you are saving overall offsets this difference. And one thing is for sure: it is better to obtain financing yourself through means other than a car dealer. By shopping around, you should be able to get the best deal possible. The internet makes it easier than ever to obtain car loan quotes. You can shop around in the middle of the night while sitting in your call room waiting for your pager to blow up. One site to check out is *www. capitaloneautofinance.com*, which currently offers used car person-to-person loans at reasonable rates, and even lower rates for purchasing the used car from a dealer. When financing the purchase of a car, the term of the loan should be the same length of time for which you plan to own the car—for example, if you plan to have the car for 4 years, opt for a 48 month term.

The decision of whether to buy a used car from a dealer or directly from another person is not 100% clear-cut. A dealer may be able to offer some peace of mind (because the business has a reputation to maintain), an additional warranty of some type, and other options (such as off-lease or certified pre-owned vehicles, which can be a great value). But if you've minimized your maintenance risk by choosing a car noted for its reliability, you may be able to find an even better deal by purchasing the vehicle directly from a private seller.

Places to look for used car deals include the classified ads in your local newspaper, websites such as autotrader.com and autobytel.com, and eBay. Yes, that's right: eBay. I have personally purchased one car and sold two cars on eBay without any difficulties. Conducting a person-to-person transaction on eBay offers an additional layer of security to your purchase. First, if you buy a car from some stranger who has listed a car in the classifieds of your local paper you have no recourse (other than small claims court) if the deal turns sour. With eBay, buyers and sellers are part of an online community that rates transactions via a feedback system. Thus, the buyer and seller both have an interest in conducting a smooth transaction because both wish to maintain a positive feedback rating, which would enable them to continue to do business on eBay. When looking at vehicles on eBay, check the seller's feedback rating and make sure there are no major problems (such as major complaints, etc.). Second, eBay offers a buyer protection feature that will reimburse you up to $20,000 if you don't receive the vehicle, the vehicle is grossly misrepresented, it's stolen, or has a lien against it, etc. It's a pretty good deal, and you can certainly find great buys on eBay.

Often, cars on eBay are listed with over twenty photographs so you can really get a good look at the car. And the history of the vehicle may be certified by Carfax, a company that verifies that a car has not been in an accident and is lien-free (that is, no one else still owes money against the car). You may have to drive a bit to pick up your vehicle if it's not in your same town, but the money you save could be well worth it. Car delivery is available from many sellers (especially used-car dealers who regularly sell through eBay) for an additional cost. When browsing for cars on eBay you can tailor your search results according to make, model, year, price, mileage, location, condition, etc. Some cars are sold through a standard auction format in which people bid up the price over a specified period of time (e.g. 5 days). The person with the highest bid at the end of the auction wins the vehicle. Other cars are sold through a Buy-It-Now option that allows you to purchase the car immediately without the uncertainty of an auction. Neither format is superior to the other in terms of finding the best deal. Sometimes a car will be listed in the standard auction format and the winning bidder will get lucky with a low bid. Other times, Buy-It-Now cars are listed with low prices because the seller wants to move the car quickly or the seller simply undervalued the car—either way, it can be a great deal. You just have to check frequently for these Buy-It-Nows to appear because, when they do, someone will quickly take the deal.

After reading all of this you still may not be convinced that buying a 4 year old car through eBay is the right move for you. Maybe the allure of having a brand new car is just too much to overcome and the only acceptable car, in your mind, is a new car. Well, this is not the best move financially, but if you choose to go this route here is what you will need to know.

"A New CAR!"

While not as difficult as bidding during The Price is Right's 'Showcase Showdown,' the decision of whether to lease or to buy is not entirely straightforward. A lease will most often offer you a lower monthly payment compared to the purchase of a new car. But don't let this cloud your decision-making process. Many people concentrate *only* on the monthly payment and end up getting into a very bad deal. By paying attention to the overall cost of the vehicle, you can save yourself a lot of money, whether leasing or buying.

The initial stages of purchasing a new vehicle should be identical whether you plan to buy or lease. First, decide on a vehicle that is known for reliability. Consumer Reports, once again, can be your ally here. Then you need to know about pricing. Edmunds.com and kbb.com (Kelley Blue Book) offer excellent tools for determining a car's value. You will want to know the dealer cost, as well as any rebates currently in effect that further lower the dealer cost. This knowledge will be your best friend.

You make a trip to the dealership and out runs the salesman. This is good; it means he's hungry for your business and you might stand a better chance of getting a good deal. If you've been walking around the lot for 20 minutes and no one has come out to greet you, leave and go someplace else. And rule number one is: don't let on that you're a physician. If the salesman thinks you're a "rich doctor" you will make your job of getting a good deal that much more difficult.

You look at the cars and decided to take one out for a spin. After taking the car for a test drive you determine that you'd like to proceed with the buying (or leasing) process. You look at the sticker in the window of the car and take note of the price. "I should be able to knock another $2,000 off of that price," you think to yourself. Wrong!

When working on price, NEVER *start* with the price posted on the car's window-sticker. This is precisely what dealers expect you to do. That is an artificial price that has no relationship to how much you should actually pay for the car. The bargaining method that will give you the most leverage is to start from what the car actually cost the dealer and work your way *up* from there, with the goal of allowing the dealer a 5% profit-margin. And don't fall for "undercoating rust protection" and other gimmicks. Cars are extremely well-built today and paying $1,000 for the dealer to spray some "magic" solution on the underside of your car is not a good move. In fact, this is true for all extras. When doing your research, take note of what the dealer costs for certain extras are. A salesman may try to shift the price up by pointing to certain extras that the car has and quoting you a "cost" for these extras. By knowing the real cost, you won't be taken advantage of.

Again, when purchasing a new car it is better to have your own financing in hand (just like when purchasing a pre-owned car). The dealer's incentive is to sell you the vehicle at all costs, not to get you a good deal on a car loan. The finance department at a car dealership will eat you for their snack between breakfast and lunch if you're not careful. So get your financing separately. Doing so will also give you one more big advantage: when you have a bank check already in hand, it's a lot easier to say "deal or no-deal" to the car salesperson. The dealer will think twice about letting you walk out of the dealership because you couldn't agree on a price when you have a bank-certified check in your pocket!

Leasing

Now, what about leasing? How is it that negotiating the total cost of the car is still related to leasing? Well, first a word about leasing. Leasing is literally renting. When you lease a car, you are renting the car from the dealer during the car's most significant period of depreciation. You are paying the dealer the amount of this depreciation so that you can later return the car to the dealer so he can sell it. This is not a secret that I've just revealed; it's actually explicit in the terms of the lease.

When you lease, you are renting the car according to its *capitalized cost*, which is just another way of saying "price." The monthly lease payment is determined by calculating the expected depreciation of the vehicle during the time you have it, dividing that amount by the number of months of your lease, and adding an interest rate to it (which is code-named the *money factor*). The amount of depreciation is determined by subtracting the *residual value* (how much the car is expected to be worth at lease-end) from the *capitalized cost* (the initial price of the car when new). By negotiating the capitalized cost down, you effectively lower the amount of depreciation that you are financing for the dealer, which in turn leads to a lower monthly payment for you.

But don't stop there. Pay attention to the money factor. It's of no use if the dealer grants you what you think is a victory on the capitalized cost only to have it taken away by an interest rate that is too high. Some sleuthing on the internet should give you a good idea of what a typical interest rate on a lease should be for your vehicle model, location, etc. It should be comparable to the interest rate for a new car loan. Unfortunately, it might take some algebra from you to determine your interest rate, since the dealer is not legally obligated to disclose to you the money factor. Even the money factor itself is not exactly an annual interest rate, but rather a number that just appears to be an interest rate. A money factor may be quoted as 3.0 in an effort to confuse you into thinking it's a 3.0% interest rate. It's not. The 3.0 money factor actually means 0.0030. To calculate your interest rate, multiple the money factor by 2400 (a conversion-constant). In this case, *what you thought was 3.0% interest is actually 7.2%*! You've got to be extremely careful with the salesperson.

Okay, you've almost negotiated a good deal on a lease. Now, just maintain your focus and you'll come out okay. The dealer will at the last minute point out the "acquisition fee," and other such charges. This was once an invented fee used to generate extra profit; now, many automakers actually do charge an acquisition fee or lease origination fee to the dealership, who then turns the cost over to you. Ask the dealer to waive the fee; you may get lucky. If not, shopping around may lead you to someone who is willing to absorb this fee in order to get your business. If the fee is waived, make sure none of the other costs or payment amounts change. You'll want to make sure the fee hasn't "inadvertently" been reincorporated into the contract.

One thing you will want incorporated into your contract is an adequate mileage allowance. The standard allotted amount is between 10-12,000 miles per year. If you anticipate you'll need more than that it is best to address this now. Bumping your allowed mileage up to 15,000 could save you significant money at the end of the lease, when the charge for over-limit miles can be between 15 to 25 cents per mile! So think ahead and make sure the additional mileage cost is correctly added to your agreement.

It is wise to bring a calculator when negotiating the lease. You'll want to recheck all calculations, paying special attention to the difference between money factor and your interest rate. If you sign the lease and later discover you were bamboozled, it will be your fault. Breaking a lease is almost impossible, which is another reason to reconsider your choice. Once you enter the lease, the car is yours for the entire lease-term; you can't change your mind.

If you have declined the advice to buy a used car and you've instead been driving around in your leased vehicle for 3 years, it's now time to return the vehicle to the dealer. There are a couple of options here. If you had a closed-end lease (which is the most common type), you have the option of buying the car at the guaranteed price that you agreed upon at the start of the lease. Otherwise, you can return the car to the dealership. If, on the other hand, you had an open-end lease, the final cost of the car will be the car's actual market resale value. If the car is worth more than was expected in residual value of your lease deal, you should be eligible to receive credit for the difference. If, however, the car is worth less than the expected residual value, you will owe the difference. Remember, your lease is literally payment to the dealer for the depreciation of the car. If your lease payments were insufficient to cover the depreciation, you are liable for the difference with an open-end lease.

To help determine whether it is financially smart to purchase the vehicle at the end of your lease term you can check the car's market value using one of the online sites mentioned earlier. If you have a closed-end lease and the market value is higher than the residual value in your lease, buy the car. You can then sell it outright on the market and take a profit. If the car is worth less than the lease's residual value, it's better to return the car. It would not make sense to buy the car at a price that is guaranteed higher than current market value.

When returning the car to the dealer you are liable for any damages or unusual wear to the car. Just as you should review the condition of an apartment with the landlord prior to moving out, you'll want to review the condition of the vehicle with the dealership upon returning the vehicle. Ask for a "condition report," which is a document that describes the condition of the car. In this way, you won't have to worry about receiving a bill for "damages" a month after having returned the vehicle. Without a condition report it would be your word against theirs. The condition report is your piece of evidence that the car was in good condition.

A few more general considerations:

- Do not lease a car if you expect to keep the car for a long time (> 4 years). For the long term, purchasing is likely a better deal.
- Most leases will require some up-front costs, such as down payment, taxes, etc. Plan for this ahead of time.
- Most leases have residency restrictions. If you move out of state (e.g. your internship is in Pennsylvania and your residency is in New York) you may be subjected to an extra monthly fee.
- If your leased car is stolen you will owe the difference between the car's market value (paid by your auto insurance) and the remainder of money owed through the lease agreement. This difference is covered by "gap insurance," and it's a good idea if you're leasing an expensive car and/or you live in a high-crime area.
- Always hold all documents in your own two hands and read them thoroughly before signing. You wouldn't blindly write a prescription for Percocet. Don't blindly sign any financial agreement such as a lease.

Here are a few other items to avoid when the salesperson tries to push them on you:

- Do *not* get credit life insurance from the dealer. The salesperson will try to sell this to you so that your car payments are taken care of in the event of your death. The problem with this is the dealership is the assigned beneficiary of the insurance policy. If you are going to have any life insurance, you want your loved ones as the beneficiaries, not a car dealership. It's better to have your own term life insurance policy, not a policy bought through a car dealership.
- Do *not* buy credit disability insurance through the dealership. They will try to push this by telling you how horrible it would be if you became disabled and couldn't make your car payment. As a resident, you most likely have some level of disability insurance through your hospital, and you may (and ought to) have your own private disability income insurance policy. There is no need to buy such a policy from a car dealer.
- In fact, *do not buy anything* that the salesperson springs on you during the last stages of the deal. Undercoating, etc. all have huge margins that are big profit-makers for the dealership with very little added value to you.

Hybrids

I am a personal fan of the hybrid automobile—lowered carbon dioxide emissions, lowered use of oil (foreign oil accounted for $302.5 *billion* of the U.S. foreign trade deficit in 2006), and the support of new eco-conscious technology. There is also a tax incentive associated with the purchase of a hybrid vehicle of up to $3,400, depending on the model and the total number of that model sold. Check out *www.fueleconomy.gov/feg/tax_hybrid.shtml* for details.

Of course, one of the most popular questions today regarding hybrids is: Will the fuel savings offset the higher purchase price? The "hybrid premium" is definitely real: a hybrid vehicle is more expensive than a standard vehicle. Actual fuel savings depends on the current cost of gasoline and the mileage of your current vehicle. There is an online calculator at www.cnet.com that will determine your fuel savings. Just go to the site and search for "hybrid fuel savings calculator."

Consumer Reports, in a test comparing fuel savings versus the hybrid's premium cost, found 4 out of 7 cars tested paid for their extra cost within 5 years of ownership. The full report is available online with membership at *www.ConsumerReports.org*. These calculations used a gas price of $2.45 per gallon; regular gasoline is currently well above that price, so hybrids are even better at producing savings at the pump.

Still, there is something to be said for minimizing emissions with a car such as the Toyota Prius or Honda Civic Hybrid. If the car interests you, I say "go for it." The tax break and fuel savings will just be an added bonus to lower greenhouse gas emissions and the ownership of a safe and reliable automobile.

Car Maintenance

There is a certain amount of responsibility required in owning a car. In a way, an automobile is very much like the human body. It needs food (fuel), it has a nervous system (computer-control of the engine, radio, climate-control, etc.), it has blood and lymph (oil and coolant), skin (paint), a respiratory system (air intake and exhaust system), and so on. Like human beings, regular maintenance can go a long way in preventing a larger problem down the road.

First, check the book that came with your car. It's usually located in the glove compartment. In the section titled "Maintenance" you will find a chart or sub-section that details when (i.e. at how many miles) certain maintenance procedures are recommended. This should be your guide for scheduling maintenance such as tire rotation, oil changes, air filter changes, timing belt adjustments, etc.

You need not use the dealership for routine maintenance. While a dealership is the place to go for warranty work or safety recalls, for routine maintenance a better price can almost certainly be found through an independent mechanic. To really get the best quality of work, if you are driving a less-common car (such as a Saab), it may be to your benefit to seek out an independent mechanic who specializes in that make.

Recommendations from colleagues can be a valuable resource in finding a good mechanic. Make sure to let the mechanic or repair shop personnel know that they were recommended to you by one of their other customers. They will take extra care to give you excellent service, since not doing so would risk losing two customers.

Don't worry about voiding your car's warranty by taking the car to an independent mechanic—federal law prohibits this. While warranty service ought to be performed by the dealership, routine maintenance (oil changes, tires, etc.) does not. If your car is still under warranty, just keep the receipts documenting the maintenance.

So when should you have the oil changed? Every three thousand miles? Well, the answer actually is: whenever the manual says that you should. Three-thousand miles is a figure that is promoted by oil-change franchises (such as JiffyLube), but it is not an absolute requirement. With today's oils and filters in modern engines, oil changes are normally recommended every 7,500 miles for normal driving conditions. This can get pushed back to every 10,000 miles with the newer synthetic (i.e. non-petroleum-based) motor oils. When having the oil changed, the oil filter should also be changed. Follow the recommendation of the service manual for your vehicle in terms of what type of oil to use. The "weight" of the oil (e.g. 10W30) is a measure of its viscosity. The first number represents the viscosity of the oil when it's cold (i.e. when the engine is not running). A lower number means a thinner oil that will be able to start circulating more readily upon engine startup (especially when the weather is really cold). The second number is the viscosity of the oil at engine operating temperature (212 degrees F). This higher number demonstrates that the oil thickens somewhat as the engine heats up in order to afford better protection. Many modern small cars today use 5W20. Make sure that the shop performing the oil change uses the proper weight oil.

And here's something that's on everybody's mind lately: fuel. If you are lucky enough to own a hybrid vehicle, you will be visiting the gas pump less frequently. But no matter how often you need to visit the pump, I'm sure you've noticed one thing: gas is not cheap. Keeping your tires properly inflated, keeping your engine tuned, and using regular 87 octane gasoline can help you save at the gas pump. Still, there are some folks who insist on burning super-premium gasoline in their vehicle. Unless your vehicle is a Mercedez-Benz S-Class, or some other high-end or extra-large machine, premium gasoline is a waste of money. The correct octane to use in your car is listed in your owner's manual. For the vast majority of cars, 87 octane ("regular") is the recommended variety. Octane is simply a measure of the gasoline's resistance to uncontrolled burning. In large engines with very high compression, low octane fuel might begin burning prior to the optimal time in the engine cycle. This is referred to as "engine knock." The remedy is higher octane fuel. Of course, as stated, this is really only an issue in large, high-compression engines. So use the minimum octane recommended by your car's manufacturer and save some money.

And when you're filling up, take a moment to check the air pressure of your tires, the levels of the washer fluid and coolant, and the condition (and presence!) of your spare tire. Often, spare tires require a pressure of 60 psi if they are the small "doughnut" spares (compared to standard road tires that operate around 33 psi). For the regular tires, the recommended pressure should be listed in the car's owner's manual and on the side of the car's door jam. Always check tire pressure when the tires are cold, *not* after the car has been driven fast or over a great distance, since this can skew the pressure reading.

Tires also need to be rotated according to the schedule in the car's owner's manual. Tire rotation moves the tires from front to back and from left to right in order to avoid uneven wearing of the tire tread. This extends the life of the tires and improves car handling. An independent mechanic can do this for you. When the tires do start to get worn (especially if you can see the top of Abe Lincoln's head on a penny when it is placed inverted between the treads of your tire), they need to be replaced. It is illegal to drive a car with badly worn tires; it's also unsafe for you and for other vehicles on the road that you may crash into. In addition to worn tread, other symptoms that the tires may need to be replaced include cracks in the rubber, unevenness of wear, bulges or blisters, and vibration while driving. Vibration can be caused by an unbalanced wheel or a suspension issue, but it could also be a sign of an internal problem with the tire. If you detect vibration, go to a mechanic and have the vehicle examined. If the tires require replacement, once again, Consumer Reports can offer some guidance in choosing a good tire. If you don't know where to go to get tires, I've always experienced good service and prices at Sears Auto Center.

*   *   *

For many people, a car may be the second-largest investment after their primary residence (third largest if you count the investment in your education). Careful shopping and negotiating during acquisition can save you money. Regular maintenance can extend the life of the vehicle and enhance your safety. Both are good ideas.

Chapter 8

Insurance

Insurance is there to protect you while you are making efforts to generate and guard your wealth. A devastating illness or injury could cost a fortune for treatment. Being unable to work stops your income—how can you pay your bills and save for retirement without income? If a fire destroys your house, how will you afford to rebuild? Or, you're driving to the hospital on a snowy morning and your car slips off the road and requires major repairs; do you have enough money sitting in a savings account to cover the body shop costs *and* to rent a vehicle so you can still get to the hospital for work while your own car is being repaired? Finally, what if the worst happens and you die prematurely? How will your family go on if they were dependent on your income?

In all of these cases, proper insurance can be your safety net. You will feel better knowing that there is financial backup should one of the events listed above happen to you.

We'll begin the discussion with health insurance, and move on in order of decreasing priority.

Health Insurance

Luckily, as a resident working for a hospital, you will be spared the irony of being a physician without health insurance. Your health insurance will be provided by the hospital for which you work. But there are still choices to be made and concepts that you should understand that will not only benefit you directly, but that will also be useful to you as a physician working within the world of health insurance.

The traditional model of health insurance (and the type of insurance your family may have been covered by when you were a child) is the indemnity plan. Another term for indemnity plans is "fee-for-service." With this model, the insured has total freedom in selecting a physician. There are no limitations imposed by the insurance company on who you may see. A referral is not required to see a specialist. The health care provider charges the patient a fee for services provided. This fee can be submitted to the insurance company by the physician's office, or the fee may be paid by the patient at the time of service. The patient would then submit the claim to the insurance company for reimbursement. Thus, the tradeoff for increased freedom in choice is increased paperwork and increased out-of-pocket expenses. Indemnity plans are generally the most expensive type of health insurance, and as such, are hardly ever offered by employers anymore.

Managed care became mainstream with the support of Health Management Organizations (HMOs) by the Nixon administration in 1971. The term HMO was coined by a pediatric neurologist from Minneapolis, Dr. Paul Ellwood. He and economist Alain Enthoven promoted the concept of a prepaid health plan in which health care was provided to patients from a designated health-care-provider network. Their feeling was that the fee-for-service model needed to be eliminated in order to contain rising health care costs.

With the goal of reducing costs (and generating third-party profits), managed health care became popular in an increasing fashion from the 1970's to today. Employers, who aimed to reduce costs while still providing health care coverage to their workers, led the shift from indemnity plans to managed care.

With an HMO, delivered care follows guidelines that are set between the HMO and hospitals, physicians, and other health care providers. Providers contract with an HMO. The agreement essentially states that the provider will accept discounted payments from the HMO in return for access to the HMO's patient-population. The patient (and employer) therefore gets a lower premium cost in exchange for abiding by the restrictions stipulated by the HMO. Such restrictions may include the need to have referrals to a specialist approved by the patient's primary care physician (PCP), who is often referred to as the "gatekeeper." Hospitalizations, certain tests, and some surgeries may require "pre-certification," which is prior approval from the HMO. If these rules are not followed, the patient may be directly liable for the cost of the services provided.

On a more positive note, HMOs have reportedly had a beneficial impact on preventive health care. When patients had to pay for services themselves and submit a claim to the insurance company, people were less likely to make an effort to seek-out certain preventive care interventions. With managed care, there is a new emphasis on preventive medicine. Mammograms, colonoscopies, etc. are paid for according to recommended schedules. Of course, this isn't done by the HMO simply out of a genuine concern for its members' well-being. HMOs realized that catching certain disease processes early made good financial sense.

Remember: managed care is mostly based on a *for-profit* business model. The HMO is a corporation that takes in money via insurance premiums and pays out money to physicians and hospitals, etc. for services provided. There must be money left over for the corporation to be profitable. Thus, for a system that is already stressed financially in the way that our health care system is, it's easy to see how HMOs are not the panacea that people had hoped for. Money that goes in to the system gets split up into paying for health care services, HMO overhead, multi-million dollar CEO salaries, and stock dividends.

If we wanted to maximize economic efficiency while providing quality health care coverage to all citizens, we would, in my view, have a single-payer health care system. Consider this: insurance functions upon the premise that risk is normally distributed among the insured. The insured pay into the system, which builds up money and has funds available to pay out for services to the minority of persons who require them. Yet, when there are multiple private HMOs that all stratify risk groups and aim to exclude treatment of certain conditions, we see a system that is actually designed to *not* provide care. The system is further injured by the very fact that it is not universal. Not all of America's uninsured are poor and jobless. Many young and healthy people who earn respectable incomes choose to avoid the expense of health insurance, a fact that has been highlighted by a recent proposal in the Commonwealth of Massachusetts that would require all persons who could afford it to purchase private health insurance. This proposal has been resisted by the estimated 200,000 or so young healthy residents of Massachusetts who have chosen to not spend their money on health insurance. And what does 200,000 young and healthy people avoiding health insurance do to the risk pool? It changes it (and not in a way that is beneficial to the insurance company). While healthy people may elect to go without health insurance, those who anticipate illness may seek out health coverage. This skewing of the risk pool has been termed "adverse selection," and it is a contributing factor to rising health insurance costs.

With a single-payer system, such problems would be avoided. Physicians for a National Health Program (PNHP) is a national organization of over 14,000 physicians that promotes single-payer health care in the United States. To learn more about this health care model, go to *www.pnhp.org*.

Of course, we do not have a single-payer health care system today. So as a resident, there will be some decisions to make when you select your health benefits package through your hospital.

So let's learn some more about HMOs, since this will most likely be the type of health care coverage you will have access to as a resident. HMOs come in different models, the first of which is the group model. With a group model, the HMO pays a physician group as a whole to see patients who are members of the HMO. In this model, physicians who participate can *only* see patients who are members of that particular HMO, e.g. a patient who belongs to an HMO different from the HMO that Dr. X works for would *not* be allowed to see Dr. X, even if that patient paid completely out of pocket.

The next type of HMO is the staff model. Here, physicians receive a salary directly from the HMO. The physicians may even work out of offices within a building owned and operated by the HMO. This can be a very efficient organization because everything is contained within the same physical space. Of course, this is a limiting model to both the patient and the physician. And, like the group model, the staff model is a closed system in which physicians are not allowed to see patients who are not members of the physician's HMO. This can become a problem for the patient if the patient changes employers and takes health care coverage from a different HMO. The patient may have created a relationship with his or her physician that, unfortunately, can not continue. Thus, when changing jobs, patients may be forced to find all new doctors, even during the middle of a treatment regimen!

An Independent Practice Association (IPA) is a group of physicians who contract together with each other. In turn, this association contracts with an HMO. Physicians practice out of their own offices and are allowed to see both HMO and non-HMO patients (i.e. an open system).

The most common type of HMO is the network model. Here, the HMO contracts with individual physicians, groups, and even IPAs. The physicians are not limited to seeing only patients from one HMO, and the patients benefit by having access to a broader choice of physicians.

Another type of managed care organization that is different from an HMO is the PPO, which stands for Preferred Provider Organization. The PPO is a network of physicians, hospitals, and other health care providers who have agreed to provide care to member-patients at a discounted rate. The payments occur in a fashion that is similar to fee-for-service medicine, except the choice of physicians is limited according to who participates with the PPO. There are some key differences between HMOs and PPOs. With an HMO, the use of an out-of-network provider leads to little or no reimbursement from the HMO for the services provided. With a PPO, members may seek services from an out-of-network provider, although reimbursement will be reduced. Another difference between the two is that with a PPO a patient does not require a referral from a PCP in order to see a specialist. A person with a PPO plan who chooses to see a dermatologist for his psoriasis may make the appointment and see the dermatologist directly without first having to see the PCP. Of course, a PPO is not without its own drawbacks. It is possible that the PPO may determine (after the fact) that a procedure or test was "not medically necessary" and refuse to pay for it. In this scenario, the physician or hospital may then bill the patient directly without any special pricing discount. Thus, along with greater flexibility in choosing health care providers comes increased out-of-pocket uncertainty.

And like the HMO, a PPO often requires pre-certification prior to elective surgery or hospitalization.

The third type of managed care plan is the POS—an acronym for Point of Service. The POS plan makes use of features from both HMOs and PPOs. A member with a POS plan may choose to receive care from a contained HMO system. On the other hand, the patient may choose to see a specialist directly who is not a part of an HMO—in this case the POS would operate as a PPO. Whether the patient is receiving benefits as if from an HMO or PPO is determined at the point at which they see a particular health care provider: the point of service.

By far the most common options available to residents are HMOs and PPOs. Well, unfortunately like most topics in personal finance, there is not one definitively best choice. First, examine the features of the two systems. HMOs are generally less expensive and are associated with predictable out-of-pocket expenses such as office visit copays. But the HMO relatively restricts your choice of health care providers compared to the PPO. There may be longer waits to obtain certain types of care in an HMO, and seeing a specialist requires prior approval and a referral from your primary care physician.

The PPO allows one to choose a specialist and to see that physician directly without first requiring a referral from a PCP. Along with this comes a wider selection of physicians from which to choose. But this reduced restriction on choice comes at a price: PPOs are more expensive than HMOs. On top of this, patients tend to report significantly more billing problems with PPOs than with HMOs.

In the September 2005 issue of Consumer Reports, the results from a survey of HMO and PPO participants were reported. In general, people reported higher satisfaction with the care they received from HMOs. What was particularly striking was the fact that two-thirds of PPO respondents reporting having experienced billing problems (a result that was three times as frequent as for HMO participants).

As a resident, it is probably simplest and most affordable to choose an HMO. You can pick up the latest ratings report from Consumer Reports for help. You can also check out the National Committee for Quality Assurance (web.ncqa. org) for guidance. It is probably better to choose a company that does business nationally; in this way, if you fall sick or are injured while traveling within the country your HMO will be able to more easily cover your expenses by treating you within one of their own networks in the city in which you happen to be. Finally, you can check with your state's Department of Insurance to see if any complaints have been filed against the HMOs available to you. You can find your state's Department of Insurance by going to *www.naic.org/state_web_map.htm*.

Once you've selected which HMO to go with, read the provided booklet in detail. Make sure that you understand exactly what is being offered. If you don't understand something, ask! The graduate medical education office or human resources & benefits department at your hospital will be more than glad to help you out with getting your health insurance in order.

Finally, don't forget about your teeth and your eyes. Through your hospital you may receive dental and vision coverage without even realizing it! It is critically important to have your teeth cleaned regularly so that you can avoid bigger problems down the road (e.g. root canals, extractions, etc.) and even *bigger* problems farther down the road, such as heart disease. The most common dental insurance is Delta Dental. Check to see if you have it. If so, you can find a dentist who accepts it and schedule a check-up. You don't even need an insurance card, just your Social Security number. You may still have some responsibility for payments not covered by the policy, but you should take the coverage that is there. The same goes for eye care. Spectera is a vision-care provider that many hospitals use. The benefits are generally minimal, but you can expect to get reimbursed about $40 for an eye exam and $80 to $100 towards a pair of spectacles or contact lenses. If you're going to get your eyes checked and some new eyeglasses, it makes sense to send your receipts in to your vision-care insurance company for a cool $120+ reimbursement check, so do it!

With your health insurance all tidied up, you can sleep well at night. Unless you are worried about getting injured or developing a debilitating illness that prevents you from working and earning a paycheck . . .

Disability Income Insurance

Your biggest asset as a physician is your ability to practice medicine, which in turn creates your ability to generate an income. A physician has a relatively late start at earning income compared to his or her peers. Most of us will not start to earn significant income until our mid-thirties. If we retire at age 65, and plan to live to age 95, that leaves us with 30 years to earn enough money to buy a house and live during our thirty years of work *and* during our thirty years of retirement (i.e. you have 30 years to earn enough money to live for 60 years). And I don't know about you, but I don't plan on downgrading my lifestyle when I retire! I plan to at least maintain it. Ideally, my wife Isabelle and I will be traveling and enjoying our retirement to the fullest. That's going to require some serious saving for retirement. If either of our incomes is stopped prematurely as a result of illness or injury, these goals will be impossible.

Therefore, after health insurance, the most important protection the young physician can get is disability income insurance. And yes, now is the best time to get it. You want to get it *before* you become disabled, right? And you want to have the least amount of exclusions in it; so you need to get the insurance *before* you get sick or have an injury.

What exactly is disability income insurance? If you become disabled and are unable to work, disability income insurance will provide an income to you.

But you're healthy. Is this really for you? Yes! The Social Security Administration reports that the average 20 year-old today has a 30% chance of becoming disabled prior to reaching retirement age. This is not something to leave to chance.

A person's first line of defense in the event of becoming disabled is Social Security Disability Insurance, which is available to anyone who has earned an income and contributed to the Social Security system. But the financial benefits are small, and getting through the bureaucratic quagmire can be next to impossible (in fact, most initial applications for Social Security disability benefits are denied). So, do not assume that you can fall back on Social Security in the event that you become a disabled physician. And while your hospital may offer group disability income insurance to you as a resident, the benefit will not stay with you after residency—plus, the terms of being disabled may be sub-optimal. For example, if you are a surgeon who becomes unable to operate due to a hand injury, many disability insurance plans will not pay you a benefit as long as you are able to work in some other non-surgical role. Therefore, what you really want to have for yourself is private "own occupation" disability income insurance.

Private individual disability income insurance will be more expensive than the generic plan offered through the hospital, but it's worth the price. The key is to get a policy that protects you if you are unable to work within your "own occupation." The narrower the insurance plan's definition of your occupation, the better.

As a general rule, a covered disability must be unpredictable. That is, the cause of your disability can not be caused by a previously known chronic disease. So if a surgeon has rheumatoid arthritis, she would not be covered in the event that her hands became too arthritic to operate since this would be attributable to the known chronic disease process. On the other hand, the surgeon with rheumatoid arthritis *would* be covered if she injured her hands in a car accident.

Since the cause of the disability can not be secondary to something within your past medical history, insurance companies are keen on finding out all of the medical dirt from your past. And you do not want to lie here. If you falsified your past medical history the whole insurance contract could be deemed null and void upon an investigation by the insurance company. Should you need to file a claim with the company, your history *will* be investigated. If a falsehood is identified, you will be out of luck—even if the discrepancy is apparently unrelated to the cause of your current disability.

With disability claims from physicians on the rise, insurance companies have become more aggressive in resisting payouts. One theory is that in the setting of declining physician reimbursement and increasing bureaucratic hassle, injured physicians are more apt to exit medicine by filing a claim for disability benefits instead of working through an injury or illness. Thus, insurance companies now require objective data demonstrating a disability. Forget about cashing out with a self-diagnosis of Meniere's Disease.

Still, you do want to have income protection in the event that you do suffer an objectively identifiable disability. There are a few classes of disability income insurance. The best (and the one you should obtain) is non-cancelable & guaranteed renewable. As the name suggests, your policy can not be cancelled and it is guaranteed renewable at the same premium cost and same benefit level regardless of changes in your income, occupation, or health. As a resident, you will want to buy this with the option to increase your benefit as your income increases. Generally, your total monthly benefit can not exceed 2/3 of your previous income or some other cap set by the specific policy. One of the great features of disability income insurance is that, assuming your premiums have been paid with after-tax dollars, insurance benefits are not subject to federal income tax (this does not apply to employer-sponsored disability insurance, which is one more reason to opt for your own disability insurance).

An example of a sound disability income insurance plan is the one sponsored by the American Medical Association. The AMA-sponsored Disability Income Insurance Plan is a group plan that defines "own occupation" as your "own medical specialty." A total monthly benefit is available up to $10,000 per month that is not to exceed $15,000 or 66 2/3 of your prior income when other insurance benefits are accounted for. The policy pays a benefit regardless of whether the disability was caused by an accident or an illness. If the insured is unable to perform the duties of his or her own medical specialty, the plan pays a benefit for up to 5 years. After 5 years, benefits may continue up to the age of 65 if the insured is still unable to work in any job that he or she is fit for by training and education. Further, there is the potential to receive extra funds to pay for accredited occupational rehabilitation. If the injured person is able to perform some duties via part-time work, residual benefits are available (i.e. a partial benefit will be paid by the insurer if the insured is able to generate a partial income).

The key for residents is that the future benefits level can be increased without additional health questions or another medical exam up to the age of 40. Thus, as your income increases after residency you will be able to adjust your disability insurance coverage appropriately upwards.

An important feature offered by this plan is the waiver of premiums, which means that you do not need to continue paying premiums while you are disabled and collecting benefits.

Finally, the policy is guaranteed renewable as long as premiums are paid, the physician is not retired, and the physician is not over 75 years of age (which shouldn't be a problem for you).

One more feature of disability income insurance that can affect your premium is the elimination period that you select. The elimination period is the length of time (in months) between when you become disabled and when the insurance plan begins paying you a benefit. An elimination period of one month means that if you became disabled on June 15th, you would start to receive insurance payments on July 15th. If your elimination period was six months and you became disabled on June 15th, you wouldn't begin receiving insurance payments until December 15th. The longer your selected elimination period the less your premium will be. You should elect an elimination period of at least three months and work to build up enough savings to cover your living expenses for a three month period.

I've discussed the AMA-sponsored plan because it highlights some of the points that you should look for in a disability income insurance policy as a physician. Other companies that are noted for providing good policies for physicians are Guardian and Met Life. Buying disability income insurance can be complicated, and it will benefit you to have someone on your side during this process. Consider asking your attendings or upper-year residents for a referral to a financial planner / insurance agent who they trust. A planner will be able to obtain various price quotes for you and will work with you to get the best coverage possible. And with the current insurance environment, it will help you to have someone who can decipher any verbiage in the policy that isn't totally clear. Better to do this correctly now and lock in a solid disability insurance plan that will be there for you over the following decades during which you practice medicine.

Remember, you will likely have some short-term and long-term disability income insurance through your hospital. This is a group policy for which you do not need to undergo a health evaluation and the underwriting process. Some of these plans are comparable in benefits to individual disability income insurance policies (with the exception of "own occupation" definitions—check through your human resources department for details). The problem is that when you leave the hospital you no longer are covered by that plan. If you continue to work for institutions that offer group policies, you may be okay. But if you work in a solo or small-group practice, you will likely not have access to a group disability income insurance plan. In this case, you would *need* to get an individual policy. If your health had deteriorated, you might not be insurable. This is another reason to get your own policy as early as possible. You never know what health problems might creep up on you later that could totally prevent you from getting disability insurance, or at least generate insurance terms that are not even worth purchasing (e.g. very expensive premiums for a very limited insurance benefit). In some cases, a person might be considered totally uninsurable for problems listed somewhere in the medical record that may, to us, seem minor. Even having ever taken an antidepressant (which are taken by 10% of all women and 4% of all men, according to the Centers for Disease Control and Prevention) could potentially make someone uninsurable, or at best only insurable at a very expensive rate for only minimal benefits.

Therefore, look into disability income insurance early so that you can lock in good benefits before any health problems arise. You will be financially better off for it and you may even sleep better at night knowing that you've got this protection.

Automobile Insurance

Not everyone will have a car as a resident; therefore, I've first discussed health insurance and disability income insurance, which are two must-haves. If you do have a car, auto insurance is a necessity both to be legal and to be safe.

Auto insurance is composed of three parts: liability, collision, and comprehensive. The most important of these is liability, because this is what covers expenses and damages that you cause to other property or people. In other words, if you fall asleep at the stop light and bump in to the Porsche in front of you, property liability covers the cost of the repairs to the Porsche. If the driver of the Porsche that you hit from behind complains of neck pain and needs hospitalization, the bodily injury liability component of your auto insurance pays the bills. Taking this further, liability also covers occupants within your own vehicle. If you are in a car crash and someone in your vehicle sustains injuries that require expensive treatment, your liability coverage saves the day.

Liability can carry a combined single limit, in which property damage and bodily injury coverage are capped by a single dollar amount. The more common form of liability coverage carries split limits, in which property damage and bodily injury liability are separated. An example would be 20/40/10, in which the cap (i.e. limit) per claim would be $20,000 for a single person's injury, $40,000 for >1 injured persons, and $10,000 coverage for property damage. This example is grossly inadequate. If you crumble the backside of a Porsche, repairs could exceed $10,000—and you'd have to foot the bill for the difference. And what if the driver of the Porsche that you hit from behind required cervical spine surgery? Would $20,000 cover the bill? No way! You will have to cover this difference, too. If you refuse to pay, or simply *can't* pay (which is a likely scenario as a resident), you will be sued. Your wages can be garnished (i.e. your paycheck would be tapped directly by the courts to make payments towards the amount you owe), and this would carry on into the future until your debt was repaid. Thus, your future wages are in jeopardy if you have inadequate liability coverage.

Again, the goal is to protect your earning power. If you are someone with a very low income it's unlikely that you would get sued because your ability to pay is not very great. But if you are, for example, an orthopedic surgeon, it's a safe bet that you would not only get sued, but that you would actually be a *target* for being sued. Therefore, you must have adequate liability coverage.

A good starting point as a resident would be 100/300/100, which translates into $100,000 of coverage for a single-person injury, $300,000 of coverage total for multiple bodily injuries, and $100,000 of property damage coverage. You want to have enough property damage protection to cover repairs to an expensive car. These are recommendations for residents. As your earnings and assets grow, you'll want even more coverage, such as 250/500/100. At that point, you could add on an umbrella policy, which, for example, might afford you liability coverage for your home and your car in addition to what is covered by your homeowner's insurance and auto insurance—such as $2 million of additional protection.

So far the discussion on auto insurance has only dealt with covering damages to other people and things. Where does the money come from to cover damages to your own vehicle? This is where collision and comprehensive coverage come into play. Collision provides coverage of the insured's vehicle if it is involved in a car crash—the costs of repairing the car will be paid for, minus your deductible; if the vehicle is not repairable (i.e. "totaled") the cash value of the vehicle will be distributed to the insured. A great policy would cover the cost of obtaining a replacement vehicle, not just the cash value of the previous vehicle. But, you may not want or need *any* collision protection. If you are driving an old jalopy, the insurance premium for collision coverage could cost more after a couple of years than the total value of your clunker—so in this case you could go without collision. If, on the other hand, you've leased or bought a brand new vehicle, you will want (and will probably be required) to have hefty collision protection to cover the total cost of the new vehicle.

What if that new vehicle is crushed by a falling tree? Since this isn't a car crash, collision does not pay the bills. This is where comprehensive coverage is your friend. Comprehensive protection covers damages to your vehicle that are caused by events other than a collision, and again, if you are leasing or have a substantial loan for a vehicle, you will need comprehensive coverage. Examples of events that would be covered by your comprehensive policy include fire, theft or attempted theft, vandalism, weather-related damage, impacting an animal (e.g. hitting a deer), or a broken windshield.

The premium that you pay for collision and comprehensive coverage is affected by the year, make, and model of car that you drive (which is another factor to consider when purchasing a vehicle; the Honda Civic is cheaper to fix than an Aston Martin). The cost of this coverage is also affected by the deductible that you elect. A higher deductible will lower your premium cost. Thus, to save money, choose at least a $1,000 deductible. If a big piece of hail lands on the hood of your car and dents it and the repair costs $700, you will pay the bill in its entirety. If a new hood costs $1200, you would pay $1,000 and the insurance company would pay the remaining $200. If you are in a bad car crash and your car is totaled, the insurance company would cover the cost of replacing the car, less $1,000.

Okay, so now *you're* covered by the three main aspects of auto insurance. If you hit another car, it's covered. If someone sues you, you're covered. If you hit a deer, no problem. But what if you are the one sitting at the stop light and you get hit from behind? Well, that's easy—the other driver's insurance should pay for the repairs to your car, and your hospital bill if necessary. But wait. That driver hasn't read this book. Or, he barely makes enough money to survive and he is driving illegally without any car insurance. What can you do then? Suing is pointless, since the guy has no money and there is no way you would ever recover any funds. So, once again, you've got to take the lead and protect yourself. This is done with uninsured / underinsured motorist coverage (UM/UIM), and the requirements for having this vary by state. It's wise to have, since you are protected in the event of an at-fault party having inadequate or no insurance. It also provides coverage in the event of a hit-and-run car crash. A good rule-of-thumb is to carry the same amount of UM/UIM coverage as your bodily injury liability coverage, e.g. 100/300.

Some states have attempted to circumvent the issue of assigning blame in car crashes in an effort to allay the concerns associated with other drivers on the road having inadequate or no insurance, and (with disappointing success) to lower insurance premiums and crash-associated litigation. These states have instituted "no-fault" car insurance. Unlike the typical "fault" model, in which fault for a car crash must be determined to have the at-fault person's insurance pay the bills, the no-fault policy basically has the rule of "every man for himself." In other words, you insure yourself and your own vehicle. In the event of a car crash, fault is not determined. Each driver's insurance pays for the repairs to the driver's own automobile. And unlike the traditional tort model, a no-fault consumer is not allowed to sue the other driver in the event that the victim's insurance is inadequate to pay for damages of property or bodily injury (unless the injuries are particularly severe). Personal Injury Protection (PIP) covers your own medical expenses, part of your lost wages, and even the cost of a funeral, under your no-fault policy. If you've got good health insurance, though, you can reduce the amount of PIP that you carry to save money, since PIP kicks in after your own health insurance has paid its share of the bills.

A couple of final trinkets of auto insurance include "loss of use" coverage, which pays for the cost of a rental vehicle while yours is in the shop, and "roadside assistance," which offers services such as towing if your car breaks down or runs out of gas. Loss of use coverage is good if you depend on your car regularly to get to and from the hospital. Roadside assistance is also a nice feature that is inexpensive, however if you belong to AAA or have a new vehicle, you may already have this coverage—so do not duplicate it.

Gap insurance, also known as loan or lease payoff insurance, covers the value of your new vehicle during the initial months in which you are "upside down" in terms of equity. Remember that when you drive off the lot in a new vehicle, its resale value plummets. At this point, the vehicle instantly becomes worth less than the amount that you owe against it (either via the new car loan or the lease term). If the car was to be badly damaged, the lender would not be able to recover adequate remuneration to pay off the balance owed against the vehicle. Gap insurance fills this "gap" between negative equity and even equity in the car. Gap insurance is often required by the lender of a loan for a new car, or as part of the lease agreement. Double check this so that you don't buy gap coverage twice. Do not put it past an unscrupulous car dealer to try to sell you gap insurance when you've already got gap insurance rolled into the leasing agreement. Be careful out there.

So now you know the basics about car insurance. Do not skimp on this. As a resident, there will be times when you will be exhausted driving home from the hospital—the unthinkable could happen, and you want to be covered, especially considering that your future earnings could be seriously affected if you don't have adequate protection. So, go for liability coverage of 100/300/100, and get UM/UIM coverage with the same limits. If you're cruising around in an old rust-bucket, forego collision and comprehensive coverage. But if you're driving a vehicle that has any significant value (i.e. it would hurt to have to pay to repair or replace it) get collision and comprehensive coverage—with a high deductible (at least $1,000) to lower the premium by as much as 30%. Obviously, collision and comprehensive coverage are essential for a new vehicle, as is gap insurance—just don't buy it twice!

You can check *www.esurance.com*, *www.geico.com*, *www.progressive.com*, and others for online quotes. If you have homeowner's insurance, you may be able to get a good deal by purchasing both policies from the same company, so check that out. A good credit score can further reduce your costs, as can a lack of speeding tickets (which can stay on your record for up to 7 years). Antilock brakes, airbags, alarm systems, garage parking, etc. can all lower your premium. Check with your college or medical school alumni association; you may be able to find a group discounted rate. If you've been with one insurance company for a few years, you may be eligible for a renewal discount—insurance companies like people who pay their bills and don't get into accidents, and if this applies to you the insurance company will give you a discount of as much as 15% to keep your business.

Hey, it's a jungle out there. But with your health, disability, and auto insurance in order, you're in pretty darn good shape. Just take it easy, and remember to look both ways before crossing the street.

Homeowners & Renter's Insurance

If you own a home there is another layer of insurance that you must have. And if you're renting, you may be required to carry a renter's insurance policy—if you're not required to do so, it can still be a good idea.

We'll begin with homeowners insurance, which is also referred to as HOI. This type of protection covers private homes, which includes loss of home, loss of the home's contents, and loss of use of the home. HOI also includes liability coverage for accidents that may happen at the home.

When setting up HOI, you want to have coverage for your home that is linked to *replacement cost*, not home resale value. This is important because often the cost of rebuilding from scratch is more than the cost of simply purchasing an already built home. Therefore, if your home burns to the ground and you were only covered for resale value (i.e. market value according to the assessment of homes in your area) you would likely not have enough money to rebuild. The type of coverage you should get is *guaranteed replacement cost*. This may increase the policy cost slightly, but it is the correct coverage to buy; the only exception would be if your home was not worth rebuilding. For example, if you lived in a row house you might not want to rebuild that exact property when you could just move to another comparable row house—in this case resale value coverage would be enough. Another example would be if homes in your area were exceedingly expensive. If the house burned down, you would still already own the land and rebuilding might not cost as much as buying a new house with a new plot of land—so resale value coverage might be adequate. Just be aware of these issues.

An additional point to be aware of is the effect of increasing property values. If you obtain a policy for your home according to your purchase price of the property and then property values in your area skyrocket, you may end up with inadequate coverage in the event of a catastrophe that would require you to rebuild. The *automatic inflation adjustment* feature should be added to your policy to prevent this imbalance from occurring. Of course, the previously discussed *guaranteed replacement cost* provision obviates the need for inflation adjustment.

It's important to remember that your HOI also covers items within your home. If there is a fire, in addition to property damage of the house itself you are also covered for damaged items within the home. This coverage is usually limited to 50 to 75% of the total policy face value. So if you had a $300,000 policy, the contents of your home might be covered up to a value of $150,000. This level of coverage generally only kicks in if the items are lost or injured through no fault of your own, e.g. through fire or theft. You may want to add additional coverage for specific items in order to obtain replacement in the event that you lose or break them. This type of extra protection is called *scheduled coverage*, and it involves separately listing an item and its appraised value as an extra item known as a "floater" on your policy. For example, an engagement ring might be included under scheduled coverage; if it's lost down the sink drain, its replacement (up to the previously appraised value) would be covered.

For all items covered under your policy you should make an inventory. Today, with digital cameras, this has become extraordinarily easy. You should photograph major items (e.g. computers, jewelry, paintings, furniture, appliances, clothes, etc.) and write on the back of the photographs a description, date purchased, and price. Specific items like engagement rings should have a professional appraisal to document the value.

Finally, your HOI includes liability coverage. This protects you financially for accidents that happen within your house or outside on your property. Typical liability offers $100,000 of coverage, however if you have a swimming pool (or some other feature that could potentially increase the risk of someone sustaining an injury on your property) you should increase your liability coverage to ~$300,000.

While it appears that your HOI covers a lot, there are certain events that are *not* covered, namely: "Acts of God." This refers to weather phenomena such as floods, tornados, hurricanes, etc. Also excluded is damage from earthquakes, pet damage, insect damage, sewer backup, groundwater seepage, rodent damage, damage from a continuous plumbing leak (i.e. if your sink has been leaking for a year and the floor rots, you will not be covered; on the other hand, if the pipes suddenly burst you *will* be covered), mold, etc. Certain of these protections can be obtained as separate / additional coverage.

You should consider coverage for damage caused by mold if you live in a high-humidity area where mold can be a problem. Recommended mold coverage might be for 10% of the value of your home. So if you have a $300,000 home, you should consider adding $30,000 of mold damage coverage if your house is at risk.

Protection in the event of a flood is another special situation. In fact, flood protection may only be obtained from the National Flood Insurance Program, to which access is through your insurance agent. Cost of this protection is dependent on your area's relative risk of flood. To check out your region's flood-risk go to *www.floodsmart.gov*. Your risk will greatly affect your flood insurance cost. For example, a low-risk area might only require a premium cost of ~$300/year and yield about $30,000 of house coverage and $10,000 of protection for your belongings. On the other hand, places at high risk may see a premium cost of ~$2,000/year—of course, the added cost should be associated with increased coverage, such as $200,000 of house coverage and $100,000 of protection for your belongings. One thing to take note of: when purchasing flood insurance, there is a 30-day waiting period between the time of purchase and the time at which the policy becomes effective. This prevents people from waiting until a big weather event is forecast and then hurriedly buying flood insurance.

Regarding another weather phenomenon, earthquake coverage can be obtained from the California Earthquake Authority. Such coverage generally offers replacement coverage of your house in association with a 15% deductible.

The recent tragedy of Hurricane Katrina has put the issue of hurricane protection at the front of many people's minds. To obtain protection that would cover your home in the event of a hurricane you will need to talk with your insurance agent about special beach & windstorm coverage.

And don't forget about your dog. Unless you're the "Dog Whisperer," you could be at risk of sustaining damage to your property from a dog that decides to eat your linoleum floor or, worse, the postman's leg. Standard HOI generally does not cover this. Here, an umbrella policy could save the day. As mentioned earlier, an umbrella policy offers you additional liability protection above what is covered in your standard homeowners insurance and auto insurance policies. A $1-million umbrella policy may cost about $300/year, but it just might be worth it if you are the proud owner of a "friendly" pit bull.

The different policy-types of homeowner's insurance have different code-names. HO-3 is the most common policy, and it covers all aspects of the house (i.e. structure, contents, liability). Of course, this excludes coverage for events such as earthquakes, floods, wars, etc. as previously discussed. The HO-3 policy can be upgraded from replacement cost to guaranteed replacement cost for an additional fee.

HO-4 may also be known as renters insurance or tenant's coverage. This policy affords protection such as liability in the event of an accident or injury, damage from lightning, vandalism, smoke, theft, wind, hail, etc., and some personal belongings coverage (e.g. $25,000).

For those living in a condominium or townhome, HO-6 is the type of policy for you. This covers the part of the building owned by the insured, personal property, and liability for accidents that occur within your unit. This policy is intended to fill the gap between what is not covered by the building's overall blanket policy. One extra to consider adding is loss-assessment coverage, which kicks in if the co-op has to spend money (e.g. in the event of a lawsuit or major repairs) that would require the unit-owners to split the bill and pay out of pocket.

When it comes time to purchase your homeowners insurance, like everything else, it is in your best interest to shop around. This holds true for all of the types of insurance mentioned in this chapter. Check with your state's board of insurance to see if there are many complaints filed against a particular insurance company. Check the financial status of the insurance company to make sure they will not go bankrupt and thus not be able to pay your claims. This can be checked at a variety of websites: *www.ambest.com*; *www.fitchratings.com*; *www.moodys.com*; *www.standardandpoors.com*; *www.weissratings.com*. Visit a few of these sites and make sure the ratings are congruent. One note of caution: these companies all use their own bizarre rating schemes, so pay attention to each company's specific grading scale.

Discounts may be offered for having an alarm system, dead-bolt locks, and smoke detectors (which are obviously essential anyway). There is the possibility of obtaining a discount for having your homeowner's and auto insurance with the same company, and you may be eligible for a renewal discount after you've been with a particular company for a number of years. Increasing your deductible to at least $1,000 is another way to reduce the cost of your premium. You should also know that newer homes (e.g. less than 7 years old) can be cheaper to insure than older homes. You want to obtain insurance for the best price possible while still maintaining a high level of quality—should you ever need to file a claim, you'll be glad you did.

If something does happen that puts you in the position of filing a claim, there are a few steps to be aware of. If you have a major house fire, you'll want to board up the windows and doors to prevent thieves from going through the place and stealing any remaining valuable objects. Your policy should cover the cost of the boards, nails, etc. that you will need to accomplish this. If you don't do this step and your house is burglarized you will not be covered for the associated losses.

Should thieves break into you unburned house, you should notify the police immediately. Whether or not the police are able to recover your items is not the point; what matters is that you've made the claim of theft official—the police report will come into play when filing a claim with the insurance company,

Finally, do not work with a public adjuster (the person who may come up to you after a fire to offer his or her services in negotiating your claim with the insurance company) until you've already had a failed attempt at dealing with your insurance company directly. If you've avoided doing business with a complaint-prone company by doing your homework ahead of time, you may likely have a good experience directly with your insurance agent without the need to employ the services of a public adjuster.

Hopefully you won't ever have to go through the nightmare of losing your home or suffering a major theft or accident at your property. But since your home is your single largest investment, it makes sense to have the proper coverage in case such events do come knocking on your door.

Life Insurance

You've insured your health, your car, and your house. Now it's time to insure the least important aspect of your life: your life. Just joking. Obviously, it's not the least important part of your life (although as a resident you may get the feeling that your superiors *do* think your life is unimportant). But in terms of priority, life insurance for a resident is the last one on the list. You must have health insurance. You must have auto insurance if you have a car. You must have disability insurance. And you must have homeowners insurance if you own a home. But life insurance may not be essential to you as a resident, especially if you are single and/or have no children. When you buy life insurance, you are basically buying insurance that gives money to those around you who would inherit your bills upon your death. If you don't have anyone around you to inherit your old bills, you don't need life insurance—concentrate instead on good disability insurance and investing in your retirement accounts. But if you have a spouse who may depend on your income, or who would have to pay a mortgage suddenly on a single income, you need life insurance. If you have children who you plan to send to college someday, you need life insurance at least to cover the cost of their educations since you can't pay tuition bills from the grave without life insurance. And while this is a morbid subject for sure, there is one piece of relatively good news: when you die, government student loans are forgiven, i.e. your spouse won't be left with a $200,000 bill for your medical education—your federal student loans (this includes a federal consolidation loan) will simply become dust in the wind.

But for the bills that will remain (such as the mortgage and *private* student loans), there is life insurance. I think the only reason it's not called "death insurance" is because it takes an already morose subject and makes it even worse. The fact is that life insurance pays a benefit to your beneficiaries in the event of your death, be it from a disease process or from an accident. The payment is named, apropos this topic, the *death benefit*. The death benefit is not paid if you die as a result of war, you commit suicide within the first two years of opening the policy, or if you are found to have reported fraudulent data on your insurance application (such as failing to mention the known berry aneurysm in your brain) that is discovered during the two-year contestability period after opening the policy.

The beneficiary is the person who receives the policy's payment upon the insured's death. Usually, the insured person may change who the beneficiary is freely. There are, however, some types of policies that list an irrevocable beneficiary. In this case, both the insured and the beneficiary must together consent to change the assignment of the beneficiary.

Like disability insurance, application for life insurance involves reporting medical history, and it may even require a policy-specific physical examination and laboratory workup. After the policy is initiated there is a two-year contestability period. During this time, the insurance company has the right to perform a thorough investigation of your application, medical history, etc. If falsified information is found within this two-year period your insurance policy will at worst be nullified; the better scenario is that you will just be charged a higher premium.

Assuming you won't lie on your application, there will be bills to pay. You may wonder how the insurance company determines how much to charge different people for their life insurance coverage. Well, if you thought forensic pathologists had a dreary job, consider the work performed by actuaries. These are mathematicians who use probability and statistics to construct mortality tables (called actuarial tables) that can estimate a person's life expectancy based on various factors such as age, gender, tobacco use, weight, etc. From this, the insurance company can predict the likelihood of having to make a payout within a certain time-frame and, thus, charge you the appropriate premium.

Premiums become more expensive the older you are, since the likelihood of dying increases with age (duh). In addition to your age, the insurance company collects data about you to compare to the actuarial tables that allow it to attempt to predict the future. The process of collecting this data in order to estimate your insurance risk is called *underwriting*. Again, this is where health and lifestyle questions are asked. And it pays to be honest, since dishonesty can nullify the whole policy as stated above. Don't think that you can get away with a fib, either, because the *Medical Information Bureau* (MIB), which is Big Brother for the insurance industry, has been keeping its eye on you (and everyone else, too) who has ever applied for individually underwritten insurance. This group, established in 1902 in Massachusetts, reports information to insurance companies such as your credit history, driving record, history of engaging in hazardous activities, and health history. A report with the MIB may be generated when you apply for insurance. Like your credit report, if you have an MIB report it remains active for 7 years. The MIB states that most people actually do not have an MIB file and that only about 20% of insurance applications generate a file. It is possible to obtain a free copy of your MIB report by calling 866-692-6901. If a report is not on record for you that does not give you the green light to skip over important facts in your insurance application. Remember, the insurance company *wants* to find reasons to charge you more money and they *want* to find exclusions to write into your policy. They may have you sign a waiver that allows them to review your medical records—if something turns up there that you didn't report, it's all over. Then you probably *will* have an MIB report that lists these conditions as well as the fact that you fraudulently applied for insurance recently. Try to get a good rate then!

If the insurance company hasn't uncovered any dark medical secrets, you will next be *rated*. This involves categorizing you according to perceived risk.

There are four basic categories. The first is "preferred best," and this is the category in which you want to be: it is for the healthiest individuals in the general population without any past medical history, who take no medications, and who do not have a family history of various maladies such as diabetes, cancer, or heart disease. Of course, very few people fit into this category. The next best category is "preferred," which includes people who may take a medication and may have a positive family history for something in the aforementioned list. Most people will fit into the "standard" category, which includes people who take a medication, may have a minor past medical history, and who have a positive family history of the previously listed diseases. The worst category is self-explanatory and is termed "tobacco." A lab test for cotinine (a metabolite of nicotine that can persist for a few days after smoking) may be used to assess an applicant's smoking situation. Beyond tobacco use, there are certain medical conditions that could cause you to be deemed uninsurable, but this is unlikely if you are young and healthy enough to work as a resident.

The process of underwriting and getting the best quote possible can be a tricky one. This is where having an insurance agent on your side is a big deal. This person will explain unfamiliar lingo and will hopefully offer support of your application. For example, if you once went to the emergency department complaining of chest pain and it was diagnosed as nothing more than GERD, the insurance company may still come back and exclude heart-related death. Obviously this is absurd, and you will want your agent to mediate addressing this issue. With a couple of letters and a note from your physician, such a situation should be able to be resolved.

Okay, so you've got your policy and you've been making your payments. What actually happens if you die? Well, first the insurer will want proof of your death—this can be accomplished by providing a death certificate or a notarized claim form. Once the death is verified, payment can be made to the beneficiary. This payment can be either as a lump sum or as an annuity (i.e. regular payments over a certain period of time). Be aware that if you had a particularly large policy and if you suffered a suspicious death, the insurance company will delay payment until they have adequately investigated the cause of your death.

How much your beneficiary gets depends on how much coverage you purchased. Some experts recommend buying a policy that is worth 6 to 8 times your annual income. So if you make $40,000, you could get a policy for $320,000. Others recommend going as high as 20 times your income, which would require a policy worth $800,000. The reasoning behind the 20-times figure is that the death benefit could be taken as a lump sum and invested in a very conservative and safe vehicle that yielded an annual return of 5%. On $800,000, a 5% annual return would equal $40,000, which was your initial $40,000 salary. You should go with the higher salary-multiple if you have children. If you purchase the right type of policy, it should be affordable to you since you will likely be purchasing it at a relatively young and healthy age.

What type of life insurance should you buy? There are different kinds of life insurance, the most common being "term" and "permanent" life insurance. Permanent life insurance is the more expensive of the two. It builds a cash value that will eventually be paid out. On the other hand, term life insurance does not build a cash value—making it much cheaper to acquire. For this and other reasons, term insurance is the most appropriate life insurance for a resident.

Think of term life insurance as an insurance policy that functions similarly to your auto insurance. You pay your auto insurance premium regularly and, in turn, receive insurance coverage for your car. If you get in a wreck, the insurance pays. If you do not crash your car, there is no payout from the insurance. Term life insurance functions in a similar fashion. You pay the premium and if you die during the insured time frame (i.e. the "term") your beneficiary receives a cash payout. If you do not die, the insurance does not pay any money. Since the likelihood of you dying during the term is relatively low, the total number of claims the insurance company must pay in relation to the number of insured who do not die is quite low. Therefore, term life insurance can be less expensive to you and still financially viable for the insurance company.

As a resident, term life insurance makes sense because, assuming you are in good health, you should be able to lock in a good rate for a number of years (e.g. 20) through what is called "level term" life insurance. You have the option of extending your coverage after the 20 years if you wish by paying an adjusted premium. Level term life insurance is a good deal because your premium is fixed for the entire term. On the other hand, annual renewable policies (i.e. one-year terms) are the cheapest at the very onset, but rise in cost each year. Since the overall costs for term life insurance are low to begin with, it makes sense to lock in a rate via level term life insurance. For example, a $500,000 level term life insurance policy could be had for as little as $35 per month for a 20 year term. And once the initial health survey has been completed, you will not be required to undergo additional health testing within the term. This is great—even if you develop a serious illness and become "uninsurable" in the sense of being able to purchase a new policy, you will keep your current term life insurance as long as you continue to make your payments.

Let's recap how term life insurance pays a death benefit to your selected beneficiary. It's simple. If you die within the term of you insurance policy the insured amount will be paid to your beneficiary. If you do not die within the term of the policy, nothing happens. No money is paid to you. It's just like auto insurance. If you *don't* get into a car crash your insurance company *doesn't* refund your money—this makes sense.

A word about suicide. Hopefully this will never be a factor, but suicide within the first two years of opening a life insurance policy is not considered an acceptable cause of death. A person can't purchase a $2-million policy and then commit suicide with the expectation that the beneficiaries will make money. This not only protects the insurance companies, it also protects people from having insurance policies taken in their name only to be killed in a fashion that is made to look like suicide. After two years, however, suicide is not excluded; therefore, a death benefit would be paid to the beneficiary of someone who committed suicide over two years after initiating the life insurance policy.

So, term life insurance should keep you covered as you are starting out as a resident and into the first few years after finishing residency. Eventually you may consider some of the other types of permanent life insurances as ways of investing for retirement and protecting the value of your estate upon your death. But this goes beyond the scope of this book. At that point, you should seek the services of a financial planner to help guide your wealth and estate planning.

You will likely have some form of group life insurance coverage through your hospital. Fill out the forms and assign a beneficiary. But the value of this group policy may be limited to your annual salary (in other words, if you make $40,000 per year, your group life insurance policy would have a death benefit of $40,000). A group policy would certainly help in the event of your death in terms of paying funeral costs, etc., but it is definitely not sufficient to offer future support to your surviving dependents. For this reason, you should seriously consider purchasing level term life insurance if you have a spouse and/or children.

*   *   *

It's easy to assume that, as a young and healthy person, insurance is not something that you need right now. It's true that you may not *need* it right now, but right now is the best time to obtain the most desirable rates and terms of coverage. With the information that you've just learned about insurance, you will definitely have a leg up over most other people who sit down with an insurance agent to discuss options for the first time. In the truthful words of GI Joe, "knowing is half the battle."

Chapter 9

Taxes

President Franklin D. Roosevelt stated: "Taxes, after all, are the dues that we pay for the privileges of membership in an organized society." While I think he was absolutely correct, this realization certainly does not quell the pain that is felt by so many as taxes become due each April.

As a resident, the pain you feel from taxes now will be *much* less than what can be anticipated in your future. Of course, this is a good thing—having a high tax bill is a privilege that many people would envy, since it relies upon a high income. The difference is that, as a resident, your taxes are deducted automatically from your paycheck. Once you become an attending and your earnings increase, you may have to start paying estimated taxes on a quarterly basis throughout the year. But that's a few years from now. Let's focus on the topic at hand, which is understanding, optimizing, and filing your taxes during residency.

The hospital will deduct money from your paycheck automatically to pay for your taxes. If you look at your paycheck, you will see the amounts listed as deductions for "this period" and for "year to date," or YTD. The first deduction is probably for FICA, which is the Federal Insurance Contributions Act. FICA is Social Security. The deduction for FICA is a payroll tax. Both the employee and employer are responsible for paying this tax. As a resident, you will pay 6.2% of your gross income (up to a limit of $97,500 in the year 2007) towards FICA. Your employer will also contribute an equivalent amount to FICA on your behalf, which brings the total amount sent to the federal government equal to 12.4% of your gross income (but remember, your share is only the 6.2%, unless you're self employed, in which case you pay the whole 12.4% because you are both the employer and employee). And we're just getting started.

The next deduction is likely Medicare. Obviously, this pays for Medicare. This tax is 1.45% of your gross income, with no upper limit. Again, your employer kicks in another 1.45%, bringing the total tax to 2.9% of your gross. After residency, if you are in a small group or solo practice situation, you will be paying the whole 2.9% tax yourself.

We haven't even gotten to the federal *income* tax yet. What is the meaning of all of this? Well, in a (successful) effort to pull the country out of the Great Depression, President Franklin D. Roosevelt established the New Deal. One of the key elements to this plan was Social Security, which was (and still is) federally mandated insurance that would provide some level of benefits in the event of injury-induced disability or congenital disability (e.g. severe mental retardation), unemployment, and retirement. It was signed into law in 1935. Prior to this, there was no real safety-net to help people who became disabled or who were born too ill to ever work. And retirement planning and saving was not something the proletariat was having great success with. Thus, one of the great accomplishments of our organized society came to be.

Of course, this achievement didn't transform the United States into a utopia. It became obvious that some level of health care provisions were necessary for our retired and disabled citizens. For that, President Lyndon B. Johnson signed Medicare into law on July 30, 1965, as an amendment to the Social Security legislation. Medicare assists in the payment of hospitalizations and nursing home services (Part A), office visits and durable medical equipment (Part B), and now prescription drugs (Part D) after the signing of the Medicare Prescription Drug, Improvement, and Modernization Act, which was signed into law by President George W. Bush in 2003. While Medicare certainly has its issues (related mostly to funding and reimbursement), it is another piece of the fabric that contributes to an organized society. We should not let current funding concerns overshadow the fact that it serves a major role in our society by providing health care to our retired and disabled population, since we currently lack an alternative mechanism for so doing.

Today, a person is eligible for Medicare if he or she (or that person's spouse) earned a taxable income for at least 10 years, is at least 65 years old, and is a U.S. citizen. A person may also qualify for Medicare benefits by being disabled or having end-stage renal disease. And while this may look like you don't benefit at all from Medicare at this stage in your life, nothing could be further from the truth. Medicare pays for graduate medical education across the United States by directing funds to your hospital, which then uses the money to support the educational machinery of your residency in addition to paying your salary—the very salary that then pays FICA and Medicare taxes and federal income tax.

Your federal income tax is also withheld from your paycheck by your employer. The amount withheld is affected by the number of exemptions claimed on your W-4 form. You also list your filing status, either single or married, on this form. Claiming a higher number of exemptions means less money will be taken out of each paycheck; claiming less exemptions causes more money to be withheld. Ideally, you should set the number of exemptions so that the appropriate amount of tax is withheld annually (i.e. you do not want a huge refund every year, nor do you want to owe a huge tax bill in April). It's better to not lend the government extra money that you could be using in your day-to-day life or through your savings and investments. Likewise, it's better to not get slammed with a large bill just as Spring rolls around. There is an online withholding calculator at *www.irs.gov* that can help you estimate the optimal number of exemptions to claim. Claiming '0' would cause the most money to be withheld; '1' (i.e. yourself), '2' (i.e. yourself and your spouse or child), etc. cause progressively less money to be withheld from each paycheck. If you are moonlighting and receiving separate, untaxed paychecks, you may want to claim '0' exemptions to buffer the tax you will owe on your moonlighting earnings. While these earnings probably won't move you into another tax bracket, they can add up to a hefty tax bill if you're not careful.

So how do tax brackets work? Tax brackets are categories of income levels that progressively increase the percentage of your income that you owe in tax. Another way of looking at this is that the tax *bracket* is the percentage of tax that you are charged on the last dollar that you earn during a year. Your tax *rate* is actually lower than your tax bracket (unless you have an income that is less than $7,825 for the year 2007). Let's see how this is so.

First, tax brackets range from 10% to 35%. Most residents will fall into the 25% tax bracket, which currently includes annual incomes within the range $31,850 to $64, 250. Falling within this tax bracket does not mean that you owe 25% of your income. Actually, the tax is assessed at the appropriate percentage incrementally, starting from zero dollars and working up to your final annual income. In other words, if you make $40,000 per year your tax bill is *not* $10,000—it is actually $6,424.25. This figure is arrived at by taxing the first $7,825 (the upper limit for the first tax bracket) of your income at the 10% rate. Your next dollars earned, up to $31,850 (the upper limit for the second tax bracket), are taxed at 15%. Finally, your remaining earned dollars above $31,850 are taxed at your tax bracket rate of 25%. If you earned enough to move into the next tax bracket, your dollars earned beyond $64,250 (the upper limit of the 25% tax bracket) would be taxed at 28%, and so on—up to the 35% tax bracket for those with annual incomes beyond $350,000. Tax bracket specifics can be found at *www.irs.gov*.

The percentage described by your tax bracket is referred to as your *marginal rate*. When calculating tax savings (e.g. what are your tax savings when contributing to your 401k plan) you should always use the marginal rate, since your savings come off the top of your earnings. Thus, a $1000 contribution to your 401k sees a 25% tax savings—it's as if the contribution only cost $750 in out-of-pocket terms (excluding state taxes).

The same holds true when predicting the amount of tax you will owe on additional income. For example, if you moonlight and are paid directly without any taxes withheld, you can use your marginal rate to predict tax owed. Therefore, a $1000 moonlighting shift really is only going to net you $750 after federal income tax is accounted for. Add an average 6% state income tax, and that total drops down to $690.

While no one likes to see their income reduced, there are cases where monetary reductions can be desirable, namely: tax deductions. Tax deductions reduce your tax liability by reducing your *adjusted gross income* (AGI), which is the amount of money on which taxes are assessed. If you make $40,000 in a year and take a standard deduction of $5,350, your AGI will be $34,650. Thus, you will owe taxes on $34,650 of income, *not* on $40,000 of income.

The standard deduction is the default "freebie" from the U.S. government that will probably be the correct choice for most residents. For a single tax filer the standard deduction for the year 2007 is $5,350. For a married couple filing jointly, the standard deduction is $10,700. The alternative to taking the standard deduction is to file itemized deductions. Itemized deductions can reduce a person's tax liability if that person has been paying sizable mortgage payments or significant medical bills, among other things. For this reason, most residents will find the standard deduction grants them the biggest tax savings. Tax software or a tax preparer will easily determine which type of deduction is the correct one for you.

Unfortunately, during the history of taxation and tax deductions, people have been engaged in maximizing deductions to the point that certain individuals with great wealth actually paid very little to no tax as a result of their tax-deduction virtuosity. To put a stop to this, the *Alternative Minimum Tax (AMT)* came out of the Tax Reform Act of 1969. Originally aimed at catching taxes from only a few very wealthy households, the AMT, as a result of not being indexed to inflation (i.e. the income limits have not increased in accordance with inflation over the years), more and more middle-income people are finding themselves owing this tax. The Congressional Budget Office predicts that greater than 34% of people who filed taxes for 2006 with incomes between $50,000 to $100,000 will have been subjected to the AMT.

So what does the AMT do exactly? Well, it essentially disallows many of the commonly applied tax deductions, such as certain medical expenses, certain tax-exempt incomes, the standard deduction, and even state and local taxes. In other words, if you end up owing the AMT, you basically become ineligible to take the above-mentioned tax deductions (and others not listed here).

The issue of more people falling within the grasp of the AMT is not something that is likely to just go away, mainly because the AMT is a big money-maker. The Center on Budget and Policy Priorities reports that repealing the AMT would cost between $800 billion to $1.5 trillion in lost revenue over the next ten years (depending on whether previously legislated tax cuts are renewed or are allowed to expire). As you can imagine, the legislature is not eager to relinquish upwards of a trillion dollars! Thus, you can plan on having to calculate whether you are subject to the AMT as you are filing your taxes.

A person may begin preparing their taxes around mid-January each year. To proceed, one needs to have received the W-2 form (i.e. the wage and tax statement) from one's employer. This form lists income earned and taxes withheld (FICA, Medicare, federal, state, and local, as well as some other required information). If you've done any moonlighting, you will also need to wait for form 1099, which lists miscellaneous income. When you list your moonlighting earnings, they will be filed under Schedule C (to report profit or loss from business), since as a moonlighting physician you are considered an individual contractor. As such, you may be eligible to deduct things like the use and depreciation of your car if you use it to drive to the hospital, etc. from your moonlighting earnings, thus decreasing your tax liability.

The last forms you will need before beginning are your bank and investments earnings statements and documentation of mortgage interest paid, if applicable.

I have always prepared my taxes using the online software TurboTax (Intuit, Inc.). Once the above-mentioned forms are in hand, it's just a matter of following the online prompts and copying numbers into the appropriate boxes on the computer screen. The software does a great job of assessing potential deductions and checking for errors (it also determines whether you are subject to the AMT). The ability to file electronically makes the whole process even easier. You can have a refund transferred into your checking account via direct deposit. If you owe tax, you can easily print out the required tax form and mail it in with your check. Overall, I've found this to be the easiest and most efficient way to file my taxes. H&R Block also now has web-based tax preparation software that looks to be quite good.

If your tax situation is unusually complex (e.g. you have a large mortgage, have had very high medical expenses, have a trust fund, etc.) you may benefit from professional assistance with your tax preparation. Ask upper year residents or your attendings for tax-preparer recommendations. When you visit this professional, make sure to tell them that you were referred to them by your colleague Dr. So-and-so; like physicians, financial professionals rely heavily on referrals and on keeping their clients/referrers pleased.

Once the tax forms are completed, make sure to print out a copy and keep it in its own file for that tax year, along with any receipts that you may have used if you itemized your deductions. You want to have all of this documentation on hand in the event of an audit.

An April 16th, 2007 article in the New York Times by David Cay Johnston titled "I.R.S. Audits Middle Class More Often, More Quickly", notes that there has been recently increased scrutiny over tax returns filed by the middle class. The number of audits on this group doubled during the period from 2000 to 2006. Further, those filing Schedule C earnings (such as moonlighting funds) were three times more likely to undergo a tax audit.

This isn't the end of the world. Most "audits" may amount to a letter from the IRS that requests more information or documentation, which can be answered likewise by a letter. In rare instances, the IRS will request a face-to-face meeting. This type of audit is cause for more concern.

In the event of a face-to-face audit, it is recommended that you obtain the services of a tax professional to help you. This will benefit you in a couple of ways. First, you can have this representative meet with the IRS agent in your absence, which effectively prevents you from blurting something out during the meeting that could be self-injurious. Second, your representative may not be able to answer all questions completely, which would require him or her to communicate with you and to get back to the IRS. This affords you time to get information and thoughts together in an organized fashion so that your response to the IRS can be as cogent as possible.

If you have the appropriate documentation that supports what you have filed, then there is no need to worry. If you don't, you will likely be charged for taxes owed. Pay the tax and you are done. The good news is if you are audited and found to not have any problems you may actually have decreased your chances of a future audit. So keep your records, receipts, statements, and file honestly.

By following the above points, tax time will not be the nightmare that many people make it out to be. In fact, "it won't hurt a bit."

Chapter 10

Finale—Keeping track of it all and moving forward into the future

With all of the information we've reviewed in this book, you may be wondering how a person can keep accurate records of everything—especially when your time is limited as a resident. Well, it's actually much easier than you think.

First, sign up for the direct-deposit of your paycheck. Does anybody even receive a paycheck that they need to manually deposit anymore? They shouldn't. The key with keeping track of your finances is to automate as many tasks as possible. Obviously, the best place to start is the beginning, and that means having your earnings appear automatically in your checking account every two weeks. Setting up direct deposit is effortless; all you need is a cancelled check and a form that you submit to your human resources department. Depending on when in the pay-cycle you sign up, there may be a check that you do need to manually deposit before the direct-deposit function is initiated.

Once the inflow of your salary is automated you can start automating the outflow (i.e. paying bills). Practically all major banks offer an online bill payment feature, and this is a great way to keep track of your bills and pay them easily and quickly. First, you need to have online access to your checking account. Next, set-up the online bill payment according to the bank's instructions. Here you will enter the name of a payee and the account number you have with that payee, etc. You can go so far as to have certain bills paid automatically each month, such as a cable bill or phone bill.

Next, to pay for items such as groceries, gasoline, clothing, etc., I suggest using a single no-fee credit card or a charge card—just make sure to pay the bill off *in full every month!* My wife and I use the American Express Rewards

Gold Card. This is a charge card that doesn't have a pre-set spending limit. The bill must be paid off in full each month. Awards accumulate as a result of your spending, and you can redeem these points either for cash or merchandise (e.g. iPod, cruise, golf clubs, etc.). One of the greatest benefits is purchase protection, which affords extended warranties and replacement of an item if it is stolen or damaged, rental car protection, emergency assistance while traveling, and even early access to concert tickets. The biggest benefit is having all of your expenses neatly accounted for in one place. At year's end, American Express will send you a summary report that details how you've spent your money; the report is broken down by categories and monthly cash-flow.

But to really keep track of your cash-flow you should use a personal finance program such as Quicken (Intuit, Inc.). You can keep track of all of your assets and liabilities including credit/charge cards, checking account, savings account, IRA/401k, student loans, private loans, etc. It may take less than an hour to set up the program the first time you use it, but it's time very well spent. Once set up, you can perform automatic online updates simply by pressing a button and typing in your "PIN vault" password. The program will download all banking, credit card, and equity transactions for you. You can set up specific categories for spending and income according to your own needs. You can even generate detailed graphs and charts (if you are so inclined).

Of course, you don't want to have all of your financial information stored *only* in cyberspace, so you should also have a paper filing system in which you keep you tax forms, year-end statements, and all other important papers (such as student loan statements, insurance documents, the title to your car or house, etc.). Optimally, really important papers should be kept in a fire-proof safe. There is a great article that is available through consumerreports.org titled "All that paperwork: what to keep and what to toss" that is available for free. Just go to the website and search for the article's title.

Conserving Money

One of the best ways to accumulate wealth is to not waste it. Despite what television and magazines will have you believe, I'm here to tell you that it's *really cool* to be frugal. This doesn't mean that you have to live the life of a Tibetan monk—it just means you have to keep control of yourself when spending money. This can be simple and can make a real difference. For example, if you're renting an apartment, don't feel obligated to rent the biggest, nicest apartment that you can afford. Instead, take on the challenge of finding the apartment that is as affordable as you can find while still offering the quality that you want. This may mean simply living in a smaller apartment within a nice building as opposed to a huge apartment in a nice building. You can also save money by conserving electricity, such as by using compact fluorescent light bulbs (CFLs) and turning lights off when not in a room. Drive a fuel-efficient car to save on gasoline and don't spend money on premium gasoline if it's not required by your car. Buy clothes on sale and only when you need them, not as an impulse to simply cure boredom. In fact, if you really want to avoid unnecessary purchases, don't make it a habit to go to the mall for weekend recreation—go hiking instead. And you may have heard of financial planner David Bach's "latte factor," which is the amount of money people spend in a day on small items like cafeteria food and lattes. Bring your own lunch if possible (or at least make use of hospital provided meal vouchers if available). And do you really need the $4.00 venti mochachino everyday from Starbucks? Try a regular coffee instead and add cocoa powder—it's pretty tasty and a whole lot cheaper.

There are plenty of ways to cut down your spending and to still live a full life. Just Google "frugal" and you will find a bunch of sites that offer myriad ideas for saving money.

CME: Continuing Monetary Education

This book is meant to be a missive to fellow residents that provides guidance in the convoluted arena of personal finance. Having read up to this point, you are now many orders of magnitude above most of your colleagues in terms of their financial knowledge. But this is just the beginning. As you continue your life in medicine and your income rises and your life becomes more complex (spouse, kids, house, sizeable investments, airplane, etc.) you will need to expand your knowledge even further. For example, you will probably eventually need the services of an account and/or tax attorney. You may also need the help of a financial planner as you begin increasing your investment portfolio and you start running into tax planning concerns. In addition to referrals from people you trust, you will want to have your own body of knowledge so that you can make your own evaluations of the professionals who you will be involving in a very personal and important part of your life.

Think of this book as the personal-finance equivalent to a USMLE review book. Great for getting key points and scoring well on exams. But once you start to specialize, it's time to read an actual textbook. Out of the 30 or so finance books that I've studied thus far, there are three that really stand out as being superb and highly appropriate for residents; I think that these books are essential to starting your personal finance CME.

The first book I'd recommend is *Making the Most of Your Money*, by Newsweek columnist Jane Bryant Quinn (ISBN 0-684-81176-6). This monumental tome is over 1,000 pages long, so it's not something that you are going to sit down and read cover-to-cover, but it should serve you extremely well as a reference book. It goes into extreme detail in a variety of topics, especially insurance, mortgages, and taxes.

Next, for the individual who wants to really understand index mutual fund investing and asset allocation, read *The Four Pillars of Investing*, by William Bernstein (ISBN 0-07-138529-0). Dr. Bernstein (yes, he's also a physician) has written a book that I simply could not put down—and it's about the history of investing, the theory of the efficient market, and coming up with the optimal balance between risk and return using proper diversification and index fund investing. He explains the elegant beauty of index fund investing and its superiority to actively managed funds in a way that is irrefutable. Not only that, but it's actually well-written and is a pleasurable read. In the words of Reading Rainbow's Levar Burton: "But you don't have to take *my* word for it." John Bogle, founder and retired CEO of The Vanguard Group, referred to this as the book he wished he had written! While this book doesn't discuss any personal finance issues other than investing, it covers its topic *perfectly*. It's a must-read; and this is one that you *can* read cover-to-cover in a few days.

Finally, another book with a relationship to physicians: *The Millionaire Next Door* by Thomas J. Stanley, Ph.D., and William D. Danko, Ph.D. (ISBN 1-56352-330-2). This book became widely known shortly after being published, and you may already be familiar with it. What you may not be aware of, though, is that the book makes extensive use of an example involving two surgeons: Drs. North and South, both of whom have an annual income of $700,000 (not too shabby!). Yet, one is truly wealthy and the other not so much. Why? The answer has to do with lifestyle and attention paid to personal finances. While one of the surgeons (Dr. South) essentially lives paycheck to paycheck (i.e. he and his family limit their spending only by the availability of funds), the other surgeon (Dr. North) manages to live well and accumulate great wealth (by living below his means and investing smartly). The book also uses other examples and affords a view of very wealthy individuals that will likely debunk the archetypal view of who the wealthy really are. The message is a simple one: live frugally and invest wisely—only by doing this can you reliably become wealthy. Plus, this is another book that can easily be read cover-to-cover.

Discharge Instructions:

Hopefully you've read *this* book cover-to-cover and you've found it enjoyable and entertaining. With the information you've learned I hope that you begin to put your finances in order and begin to build a solid future for you and your family. Remember: pay yourself first; use tax-sheltered retirement investing (e.g. IRA/401k) with indexed mutual funds or a target retirement fund; insure yourself adequately; live frugally; and continue learning, beginning with the above-mentioned books. If you do this, I'm confident that you will be well on your way to protecting yourself and your family while building the foundation for an enjoyable retirement.

References

Bernstein, William. *The Four Pillars of Investing—Lessons For Building a Winning Portfolio*. New York: McGraw-Hill, 2002.

Himmelstein DU, Warren E, Thorne D, Woolhandler S. Illness and injury as contributors to bankruptcy. *Health Aff (Millwood)* 2005 Jan-Jun; Suppl Web Exclusives: W5-63-W5-73.

Quinn, Jane Bryant. *Making the Most of Your Money*. New York: Simon & Schuster, 1997.

DeGroote R. The Economics of Managed Care Reimbursement: A rationale for nonparticipation. *Bulletin of the American College of Surgeons* April 2007: 28-36.

Fonda, Daren. "Why the Most Profitable Cars Made in the U.S.A. are Japanese and German." TIME; May 19, 2003.

Johnston, David Cay. "I.R.S. Audits Middle Class More Often, More Quickly" The New York Times; April 16, 2007.

Kazel R. CEO compensation: Accomplishments translate into healthy paychecks. *AMA News*. May 26, 2003.

Stanley TJ, Danko WD. *The Millionaire Next Door—The Surprising Secrets of America's Wealthy*. Marrietta, GA; Longstreet Press, Inc., 1996.

Contact Information

AAA
American Automobile Association
www.aaa.com

A.M. Best Company
"The Insurance Information Source"
www.ambest.com

American Express
https://home.americanexpress.com

American Medical Association
"Physicians dedicated to the health of America."
www.ama-assn.org

American Medical Association Insurance Agency
Disability income insurance
www.amainsure.com

American Medical Student Association
"It takes more than medical school to make a physician."
www.amsa.org

AnnualCreditReport.com
www.annualcreditreport.com
Annual Credit Report Request Service
P.O. Box 105283
Atlanta, GA 30348-5283

Autobytel
"Free New Car Price Quotes, Used Cars, and Auto Reviews."
www.autobytel.com

AutoTrader
"Used Cars, New Cars, Buy a Car, Sell Your Car."
ww.autotrader.com

Bankrate.com
"Comprehensive. Objective. Free."
www.bankrate.com

Bloomberg
Investing, Market Data, Financial Calculators
www.bloomberg.com

California Earthquake Authority
www.earthquakeauthority.com
877-797-4300
California Earthquake Authority
801 K Street, Suite 1000
Sacramento, CA 95814

Capital One Auto Finance
"Auto Loans, Car Loans, Auto Refinance."
www.capitaloneautofinance.com

Carfax
"Vehicle History Reports on all used cars."
www.carfax.com

Center on Budget and Policy Priorities
www.cbpp.org
202-408-1080
820 First Street, NE, Suite 510
Washington, DC 20002

Centers for Disease Control and Prevention
"Your Online Source for Credible Health Information."
www.cdc.gov

Consumer Reports
"Expert—Independent—Non-profit"
www.consumerreports.org

Delta Dental
"Everyone deserves a healthy smile."
www.deltadental.com

Dow Jones
"Dow Jones & Company Publishes the Worlds Most Vital Business and Financial News and Information."
www.dj.com

eBay
"Whatever it is . . . you can get it on eBay."
www.ebay.com

Edmunds
"Where smart car buyers start."
www.edmunds.com

Emigrant Direct
American Dream Savings Account
www.emigrantdirectcom

Esurance
"Quote. Buy. Print."
www.esurance.com
800-378-7262
Esurance
650 Davis Street
San Francisco, CA 94111

Equifax
www.equifax.com
800-685-1111
Equifax Credit Information Services, Inc.
P.O. Box 740241
Atlanta, GA 30374

Experian
www.experian.com
888-397-3742

Fair Isaac Corporation—creator of the FICO credit score
"Start managing your credit health by learning how credit scores work."
www.fico.org

Federal Direct Consolidation Loans Information Center
http://loanconsolidation.ed.gov/

Fidelity Investments
www.fidelity.com
800-343-3548
Fidelity Investments
P.O. Box 770001
Cincinnati, OH 45277-0001

Fitch Ratings
"Know Your Risk"
www.fitchratings.com

ForSaleByOwner.com
"Sell home house condo Buy Real Estate MLS."
www.forsalebyowner.com

Fuel Economy
United States Department of Energy, Energy Efficiency, and Renewable
Engery
www.fueleconomy.com

GEICO
www.geico.com
800-861-8380
Government Employees Insurance Company
One GEICO Plaza
Washington, DC 20076

Guardian
www.guardianlifeinsurance.com

H&R Block
"Taxes, Online Tax Preparation, Tax Software."
www.hrblock.com

ING Direct
The Orange Savings Account
www.ingdirect.com

Internal Revenue Service (IRS)
United States Department of the Treasury
www.irs.gov
800-829-1040

Kelley Blue Book
"New Car Prices—Used Car Values"
www.kbb.com

Medical Information Bureau (MIB)
www.mib.com
866-692.6901
MIB, Inc.
P.O. Box 105
Essex Station
Boston, MA 02112

Medicare
www.medicare.gov

Met Life
800-638-5433
www.metlife.com

Moodys
www.moodys.com

Morningstar
"Stocks, Mutual Funds, and Investing."
www.morningstar.com

National Association of Insurance Commissioners
"Making progress . . . together."
www.naic.org

National Committee for Quality Assurance
"Measuring quality. Improving health care."
web.ncqa.org

National Flood Insurance Program
www.floodsmart.gov
888-379-9531
Federal Emergency Management Agency (FEMA)
500 C Street S.W.
Washington, DC 20472

NASDAQ
The NASDAQ Stock Market
www.nasdaq.com

NYSE
New York Stock Exchange
www.nyse.com

Office of New York State Attorney General
Check for updates regarding Student Lending
www.oag.state.ny.us/

Physicians for a National Health Program
"Health Care is a Human Right"
www.pnhp.org

Progressive
www.progressive.com
800-776-4737
The Progressive Corporation
6300 Wilson Mills Road
Mayfield Village, OH 44143

Quicken
"Financial Planning, Small Business, Healthcare Management Solutions."
www.quicken.intuit.com

Sallie Mae
"The nation's leading provider of student loans."
www.salliemae.com
888-2-SALLIE (888-272-5543)
Sallie Mae Servicing
P.O. Box 9500
Wilkes-Barre, PA 18773-9500

Spectera
"Vision care benefits and vision plans."
www.spectera.com

Standard & Poor's
"The world's foremost provider of independent credit ratings, indices, risk evaluation, investment research, data, and valuations."
www.standardandpoors.com

The Student Doctor Network
www.studentdoctor.net
TransUnion
www.transunion.com
877-322-8228

TurboTax
"Online Taxes, Income Tax Software, Tax Preparation."
www.turbotax.intuit.com

United States Social Security Administration
www.ssa.gov

Vanguard
www.vanguard.com
877-662-7447
The Vanguard Group
P.O. Box 1110
Valley Forge, PA 19482-1110

Vehix
"Road Map to the Automotive World."
www.vehix.com

Weiss Ratings
"TheStreet.com Ratings"
www.weissratings.com

Glossary of Terms

- **401(k):** an employer-sponsored retirement plan named after the section of the United States tax code that describes it. Through this plan, employees contribute money on a *pre-tax* basis. The current annual contribution limit for 2007 is $15,500. Money is invested (usually in mutual funds) and investment gains grow tax-free. Often, in order to encourage employee participation, an employer offers a *match* in which money is contributed by the employer into the employees retirement account (for example, a 50% match). There are various regulations that limit how money may be withdrawn from a 401(k). Some allowable reasons for early withdrawal include funding the down payment on a first-time home; to prevent eviction; major medical bills; and other financial hardships. Money taken from the 401(k) in a manner that is not permitted is subject to a 10% early withdrawal penalty as well as federal income taxation. Withdrawals may be made being at age 59 1/2. Withdrawals *must* be made when the participant turns age 70 ½ (otherwise known as required minimum distributions).

- **403(b):** an employer-sponsored retirement plan available through educational and non-profit organizations. It is named for the section of the United States tax code that describes it. Money is contributed by the employee on a *pre-tax* basis. There may be additional contributions from the employer. The rules and regulations of the 403(b) are essentially the same as for the 401(k).

- **457:** an employer-sponsored retirement plan available through governmental employers. It is named for the section of the United States tax code that describes it. Money is contributed by the employee on a *pre-tax* basis. Generally, though, 457 plans can not accept employer-matched contributions. The rules governing the 457 are essentially the same as for the 401(k), except there is no 10% penalty for early withdrawals (i.e. before age 59 1/2) as long as the employee has separated from service with the employer under whom the 457 was offered.

- **1040:** form 1040 from the United States Internal Revenue Service is the starting form for filing individual federal income tax. Depending on the filers tax complication, various versions of form 1040 may be used. Those filing itemized deductions and/or capital gains/losses would use the standard form 1040. A simpler tax situation (e.g. no standardized deductions, no capital gains/losses) could make use of the shorter 1040A or 1040EZ forms.

- **1099:** form 1099 is distributed by the United States Internal Revenue Service to detail money earned by independent contractors other than through salary and wages. For example, untaxed earnings from moonlighting would be documented on form 1099, from which the data would be transferred to form 1040 for the filing and payment of appropriate taxes.

- **12b-1 fees:** a class of fees potentially charged for the administration of some mutual funds—includes fees to pay brokers and those who sell fund shares and to pay for advertising, the printing and mailing of prospectuses to new investors, and the printing and mailing of sales literature.

- **Actively managed mutual fund:** a mutual fund that has a specific investing goal (e.g. "aggressive growth") and is therefore managed in a way that involves actively buying and selling stocks (as opposed to a "buy and hold" strategy). As a result of the necessary frequent buying and selling of stocks, actively managed mutual funds incur additional costs related to trading fees and capital gains taxes. There are often additional expenses related to compensation for the fund manager. As a result of added fees and taxes, actively managed funds have a very difficult time outperforming index mutual funds.

- **Actual cash value:** a term often used to describe an extent of reimbursement for an insured item. For an item insured for actual cash value, the amount paid by the insurance company would equal the market value of the insured item, *not* the amount of money needed to replace the item through purchase of a new or current equivalent (see *replacement value*).

- **Actuarial table:** also called a "life table" or "mortality table," this is a table that lists the probability of a person of a given age dying prior to reaching their next birthday. This information is used by insurance companies in their calculations of predicted pay-outs, insurance premiums, etc.

- **Actuary:** Actuaries are experts in mathematics, economics, finance, probability, and statistics. They attempt to predict the likelihood of certain events occuring (such as death) and the relationship of these events to the conduct of associated businesses (such as the insurance industry).

- **Adjusted gross income (AGI):** a United States tax term used to describe the income that is assessed federal income tax. AGI is arrived at by taking one's gross income and subtracting allowable deductions. For example, a person with a gross income of $40,000 who takes the standard deduction ($5,150) has an adjusted gross income of $34,850.

- **Adverse selection:** also known as "anti-selection." It describes a situation in economics or insurance in which adverse outcomes result from asymmetries of information. For example, healthy people foregoing health insurance while illness-prone people seek out health insurance leads to skewing of the insured risk pool, which results in higher than predicted insurance payouts.

- **Aftermarket:** the buying and selling of stocks from investor to investor, as opposed to from company to investor. Also known as the "secondary market."

- **Alpha:** also called the "alpha return," this is a measure of the excess market return generated by the manager of an actively managed mutual fund in comparison to a benchmark index mutual fund. Alpha may also refer to the difference between the fair and actually expected return of a stock.

- **Alternative minimum tax (AMT):** the *Alternative Minimum Taxi (AMT)* came out of the Tax Reform Act of 1969. Originally aimed at catching taxes from only a few very wealthy households, the AMT, as a result of not being indexed to inflation (i.e. the income limits have not increased in accordance with inflation over the years), more and more middle-income people are finding themselves owing this tax. It essentially disallows many of the commonly applied tax deductions, such as certain medical expenses, certain tax-exempt incomes, the standard deduction, and even state and local taxes. The Congressional Budget Office predicts that greater than 34% of people who filed taxes for 2006 with incomes between $50,000 to $100,000 will have been subjected to the AMT.

- **Amortization:** "to deaden" in Latin. In financial terms, amortization describes the paying down of a debt through installments of payment.

- **Annuity:** a financial product that accumulates a value and then pays out a current value at regular payments (e.g. monthly or yearly).

- **Appreciation:** the increase in value of an asset as a result of a given market assigning more worth to that asset.

- **Annual percentage rate (APR):** an expression of the effective interest rate that will be paid on a loan, taking into account certain one time fees, etc. It is designed to make it easier for consumers to compare loans.

- **Adjustable rate mortgage (ARM):** a mortgage with an interest rate that changes (usually annually) in relation to its assigned index (such as United States Treasury Bill interest rates). The ARM usually charges an interest rate slightly higher than the rate of its index. ARMs usually begin with a very low "teaser rate" for the first year and then proceed to follow their assigned index. While there is the potential to save money if interest rates are low, there is also the potential to have higher required monthly payments if interest rates rise significantly.

- **Asset allocation:** dividing your invested capital among different asset classes, such as stocks, bonds, and cash reserves. The goal of asset allocation is to potentially reduce portfolio risk since in any given year it is not possible to predict which asset class will perform best (or worst), therefore by spreading your capital among different classes you reduce the negative impact from being potentially totally invested in a poorly performing asset class. Further, the different asset classes are not perfectly correlated to each other, which confers additional portfolio protection. See also *diversification.*

- **Automatic inflation adjustment:** Regarding insuring your house through homeowner's insurance, one must be aware of the effect of increasing property values. If you obtain an insurance policy for your home according to the purchase price of the property and then property values in your area skyrocket, you may end up with inadequate coverage in the event of a catastrophe that would require you to rebuild. The *automatic inflation adjustment* feature may be added to a homeowner's insurance policy to automatically adjust the insured value of your home (since property values tend to follow inflation). See also *guaranteed replacement cost.*

- **Back-load mutual fund:** also known as deferred sales charge, this is a fee you pay when you sell your shares that typically goes to the brokers who sell the fund's shares. You should avoid mutual funds that charge such fees. See *no-load mutual fund.*

• **Balance transfer:** in reference to the transfer of consumer debt, this refers to moving debt held by one institution with a given interest rate over to another institution with a preferable interest rate. An example would be moving the debt on a credit card that charges 21% interest to another credit card that charges 0% interest for 12 months for balance transfers. It is extremely important to pay the transferred balance off within the 12 months' time in order to avoid the debt being subjected to the new credit card's standard interest rate.

• **Balloon-payment mortgage:** infrequently used in residential real estate. Briefly, you may have a short-term mortgage (such as a 7-year term) during which time monthly payments are made at a 30-year rate. Obviously, this discrepancy is insufficient to cover the total cost of the loan. At the end of the term, a large final payment is due to cover this difference. This is known as the balloon payment, and it can be devastating if one is not financially able to pay it.

• **Bankruptcy:** The legal status of being judged to have the inability to pay bills. In chapter 7 bankruptcy (the most commonly filed bankruptcy) the debtor's assets are liquidated (i.e. sold) and the proceeds are distributed among the creditors in order to pay off owed debts. Certain unsecured debts (e.g. credit cards) are forgiven. In chapter 11 bankruptcy (which is mostly applicable to companies) the debtor does not undergo asset liquidation; rather, there is a reorganization of assets and debts. Some debts are forgiven and others are repaid according to a schedule as per the terms of the bankruptcy ruling. Chapter 13 bankruptcy is the chapter 11-equivalent for individuals; it allows an individual to reorganize debts and enter a scheduled repayment plan. Being able to file for chapter 13 bankruptcy relies on an individual having sufficient disposable income in order to meet the rescheduled debt obligations. It should be noted that while mishaps such as late payments on a credit card remain on one's credit report for 7 years, a bankruptcy remains on one's credit report for 10 years. As consumer debt has risen over the years and many people have found it extremely difficult to pay their bills, there has been a resultant increase in bankruptcy filings. Under intense lobbying pressure from credit card companies (which spent over $100 million in lobbying costs over 8 years), etc., the Republican Congress passed the Bankruptcy Abuse Prevention and Consumer Protection Act of 2005 on April 14, 2005. This law makes it more difficult for consumers to file chapter 7 bankruptcy (in which certain debts are erased) and instead directs more consumers to file for chapter 13 bankruptcy (in which debts are repaid over time according to a court-appointed schedule). Many critics have pointed to rising credit card interest rates and fees, in conjunction with perceived "predatory lending", as major causes of increased consumer bankruptcies. Further, this law provides for the repayment of credit card debt as a priority over the repayment of other debts, such as alimony/child support.

- **Basis:** In the setting of the United States tax law, basis (cost basis) is the initial price paid for a property (e.g. real estate, stocks, etc.). When this property is sold (either at a loss or a gain) the difference between the selling price and the basis is reported as the capital gain (or loss). The term may also refer to a *basis point*, which is $1/100^{th}$ of a percent. For example, 1% plus 50 basis points equals 1.5%.

- **Bear market:** In reference to the stock market, a bear market is a pessimistic market associated with declining stock valuations that feeds on itself in a vicious cycle. One of the most infamous bear markets occurred from 1930 to 1932, which marked the beginning of The Great Depression. A bear market will eventually level off and then cease, marked by a change to increasing prices as the market reverts to the mean.

- **Beneficiary:** The person who receives monetary payment from a benefactor. For example, the beneficiary of a life insurance policy is the person who receives the death benefit (money) upon the insured's (benefactor's) death.

- **Beta:** Also called the *beta coefficient*. This is a factor that describes the volatility of an equity in reference to a standard index, such as the S&P 500. By definition, an equity or fund with a beta of 1.0 exhibits volatility that is equivalent to the S&P 500. For example, if the S&P 500 gains 12%, the equity with a beta of 1.0 will also gain 12%. A beta greater than one signifies volatility greater than the S&P 500 (for example, if the S&P 500 gains 12%, the equity with a beta of 2.0 will gain 24%); a beta of less than 1 signifies volatility less than the S&P 500 (for example, if the S&P 500 gains 12%, the equity with a beta of 0.5 will gain 6%)

- **Bill:** A type of bond that has a short maturation period (e.g. months instead of years). See *bond*.

- **Blue chip:** Named after the most valuable chips in poker, a blue chip stock or blue chip company refers to stable, large-cap companies that have a solid history of growth and dividend payments. Examples include IBM and GE.

- **Bond:** Literally a loan to a company or municipality. The issuer of a bond agrees to repay the principal amount at a set time in the future, along with potential interest payments to the purchaser of a bond. Bonds have historically had lower returns than equities (i.e. stocks) over the past history of the stock market. However, high-grade bonds can be less volatile than equities. With many analysts predicting that bonds will have returns comparable to equities in the coming future, it is recommended that a portfolio contain bonds as part of its diversification.

- **Bull market:** An optimistic market in which increasing investor confidence is associated with a buying trend, as investors anticipate further capital gains. An example of a bull market is the performance of the stock market in the 1990s, when returns grew at their fastest pace ever in the history of the U.S. stock market. A bull market will eventually lead to a leveling-off of prices and then ceasation, marked by a price decline, as the market reverts to the mean.

- **Cafeteria plan:** a general term that describes an employee benefit plan in which the employee is able to select different specific benefits such as health insurance (e.g. HMO vs. PPO), group disability insurance, group term life insurance, and medical savings accounts.

- **Cap:** financially a cap refers to some type of upper limit. For example, an adjustable rate mortgage may have an annual interest rate cap of 2%, in which the interest rate may increase by no more than 2% within a given year, regardless of how the assigned indexed interest changes.

- **Capital:** money invested in a company; may also refer to any valuable (time, effort, etc.) used to invest into an endeavor (such as a business, etc.).

- **Capital gain:** when a holding (such as real estate or an equity) is sold for a profit (i.e. sold for a price higher than the original purchase cost, or basis), the net profit is termed *capital gain.*

- **Capital gains tax:** Capital gains are considered a form of income and are therefore subject to taxation. Long-term capital gains (from the sale of an item held for at least 12 months) may be taxed to a maximum of 20%. Short-term capital gains (from the sale of an item held for less than 12 months) are taxed at the seller's regular marginal income tax rate (e.g. 28%).

- **Capital loss:** When an asset is sold at a price less than the original price paid (basis cost), the net loss is termed a *capital loss.* Capital losses can be used to offset capital gains for tax purposes if both assets are sold within the same calendar year.

- **Capitalized cost:** the effective final "sale price" in the setting of an automobile lease.

- **Certificate of deposit (CD):** a certificate issued by a bank that indicates that a specific amount of money has been deposited. The deposited money is held by the institution for a specified period of time until the time of maturity, at which point the depositor has the money returned plus interest. Durations may be as long as 5 years, and interest rates may approach and exceed 5%.

- **Certified check:** like a cashier's check, a certified check can not "bounce." That is, when a certified check is issued by a bank, the bank sets aside the funds needed to pay the check. In this way, the recipient of a certified check or a cashier's check does not need to wait for the funds to clear. On the other hand, a personal check does not carry a guarantee that funds will be paid. Thus, a certified check is the preferred form of payment for official transactions such as paying for closing costs upon the purchase of a house.

- **Certified pre-owned:** certain automobile manufacturers offer used vehicles under the appellation "certified pre-owned," in which late model automobiles are inspected at a dealership and essentially refurbished. These vehicles may also include some type of basic warranty.

- **Charge card:** unlike a credit card, in which a balance may remain over time and accrue interest, a charge card requires the user to pay the balance off in full each month, without the accumulation of interest. An example of a charge card is the American Express Gold card.

- **Closed-end lease:** with an automobile lease, a closed-end lease specifies what the residual value of the automobile will be upon the end of the lease term. This is the most common type of automobile lease. See also *open-end lease.*

- **Closing:** the final step in executing a real estate transaction. At the closing the buyer delivers a bank check to the seller for the purchase price of the property; the deed is signed over to the buyer; a lawyer registers the new deed with the local government.

- **Closing costs:** monies owed upon the closing of a real estate transaction. Typical fees include attorney fees, title fees, surveying costs, points, appraisal fees, pro-rata insurance/tax/interest, etc. The closing costs can approach 3 to 5 percent of the final sale price of the house.

- **COBRA:** Consolidated Omnibus Budget Reconciliation Act of 1985; a law passed by Congress that requires employers to offer health insurance coverage to employees at their own cost upon leaving employment. For example, if you receive health insurance through your hospital and are finishing residency, you may elect to continue your health insurance (at your own expense) for up to an additional 18 months. This would be done if one expected a delay in resuming health care insurance coverage (such as leaving residency in July and beginning work in October). The real benefit is to continue health insurance coverage so that the new health insurance plan will not exclude any pre-existing conditions, which could happen if there is a lapse in health insurance coverage.

- **Collision:** regarding automobile insurance, collision coverage is the part of the insurance policy that pays for repairs to your vehicle in the event of a car crash (i.e. a collision with another automobile).

- **Compound interest:** essentially interest paid on previously earned interest as well as on the principal balance. In this way, compound interest allows money to grow exponentially (as opposed to linearly) over time. It is the key reason why one must begin saving and investing as early as possible. Through compound interest, the "rule of 72" can predict how long it will take for one's money to double in relation to what interest rate is being applied to the investment. To use the "rule of 72," simply divide 72 by the interest rate. For example, money earning 10% interest will double in 7.2 years (72 divided by 10).

- **Comprehensive:** regarding automobile insurance, comprehensive coverage pays for the repair of your vehicle when damage is caused by events other than a collision with another automobile. An example would be a falling tree branch that dents the roof of your car.

- **Consumer Reporting Agency (CRA):** a company that collects and distributes information about individuals that is used for determination of creditworthiness, etc. The "big three" CRAs are Equifax, Experian, and TransUnion.

- **Contestability period:** the period of time during which an insurance company my find an inaccuracy in your insurance application (such as life insurance or disability income insurance). For example, if you list that you do not use tobacco but the insurance company tests you and determines that you are a tobacco user, your rating may be changed. The contestability period is typically two years duration, after which time the policy becomes "incontestable." Once the policy is incontestable, the information used to rate the policy is permanent; if you decide to begin skydiving once the policy is incontestable the policy will not be changed, even though your risk as an insured person has changed.

- **Co-op:** short for "cooperative." A legal entity in which a residents own shares of a building or property. Examples include condominiums and town houses.

- **Cotinine:** the main metabolite of nicotine; it is detectable in urine, saliva, and blood and may be tested for by an insurance company to verify an applicant's tobacco status. It is possible for one to test positive if one has been in an extremely smoky environment even if one does not smoke. Cotinine remains in the blood for up to 96 hours after exposure to nicotine. In addition to smoking, nicotine patches and gum will cause positive cotinine test results.

- **Credit card:** a buyer uses a credit card to make purchases. Money is effectively lent to the consumer, who must then pay it back. Usually there is a grace period (e.g. 21 days) during which the balance does not accumulate interest. After the grace period the balance begins accumulating interest (which can be as high as 29.9%). Interest is capitalized to the balance monthly. The consumer has the option to make a minimum monthly payment (an amount which, if the consumer did not make additional purchases, could still lead to repayment over the course of many years at considerable additional expense through capitalized interest charges). Credit cards often have unfavorable terms, such as high interest rates, high fees for late payments, and the ability of the credit card issuer to substantially raise the card's interest rate without reason. Because of this, the consumer is well advised to pay credit card balances off in full every month or, better yet, use a charge card.

- **Credit report:** a record of a person's credit history. There are three main companies that maintain credit files on people: Equifax, Experian, and

TransUnion. Items such as credit cards, charge cards, lines of credit, consumer loans, student loans, mortgages, and addresses are kept on file. Additionally, inquiries are recorded—multiple inquiries in a short period of time can negatively affect one's credit score. The credit report also details timeliness of bill payment, the most recent balance on credit cards, the cards' credit limits, and the length of time that the accounts have been maintained. Credit reports should be checked at least yearly, as well as at least six months prior to a major purchase (such as buying a house). Inaccuracies must be reported to the reporting agency; the process of error correction can be lengthy.

- **Credit score:** created by the Fair Isaac Corporation, the FICO score is a numerical grade of one's creditworthiness, and can range from ~350 to ~850. The score is used by lenders to predict a person's predicted rate of default for a loan. The precise way in which the score is calculated remains a secret, however there are certain aspects of one's credit history that are known to affect the score. Factors that influence one's score positively include: payment of all bills on time; debt of 40% or less than one's available credit (e.g. owing $399.00 on a credit card with a $1000 credit limit); accounts that have been in good standing for a long period of time (i.e. years); few recent inquiries. Factors that negatively affect one's credit score include: late payments; high debt to available credit ratio; short credit history; multiple recent inquiries; bankruptcy. Negative events such as late payments will remain on the credit report for up to 7 years. Bankruptcy remains listed on the credit report for up to 10 years. The average FICO score in the United States is considered to be approximately 720. For sure, one should aim for a credit score of >650 in order to get acceptable loan interest rates. Generally, a higher credit score translates into better interest rates up to a point. For example, a person with a credit score of 760 would be offered a lower interest rate for a loan compared to another person who has a credit score of 650. This is not a linear relationship, though. A person with a credit score of 830 will probably not be offered a lower interest rate on a loan compared to a person with a credit score of 790.

- **Death benefit:** the payment of funds to the beneficiary of an annuity or insurance policy when the policyholder dies. The money may be accepted as a lump sum or as an annuity (i.e. regular payments extended over a set period of time). The death benefit is also sometimes referred to as the *survivor benefit.*

- **Deductible:** when a claim is made for payment from an insurance company, there is often an amount of money that the insured must first cover with out-of-pocket funds before the insurance company will pay. For example, if a person has a $1,000 deductible with their automobile insurance policy and the insured's vehicle is in a car crash that results in $5,000 worth of repairable damage, the insured would pay $1,000 (the deductible) and the insurance company would pay $4,000 (i.e. the remainder of the cost). Deductibles may also apply to homeowner's insurance and health insurance.

- **Deed:** a legal document that indicates ownership of a property; most commonly used to transfer title of real estate from one person to another.

- **Default:** in reference to payment of a loan, to default means to lapse and discontinue repayment of that loan. May also refer to one's failure to comply with other provisions of the loan agreement.

- **Deferment:** student loan repayment may be postponed under certain specific circumstances. A deferment is a postponement of repayment in which federally subsidized student loans have interest payments covered by the U.S. government. Examples of eligible deferments include "internship deferment" and "economic hardship deferment." Deferment is preferable to forbearance, in which interest payments are not made by the federal government towards subsidized loans. See *forbearance.*

- **Depreciation:** an object with a finite life will inevitably lose value over time as the item's period of usefulness comes to an end. This non-cash decrease of an asset's value is termed *depreciation*, and it can be used as a non-cash expense in accounting.

- **Disability income insurance:** provides a source of income to the beneficiary in the event that the insured is no longer able to work and earn an income as a result of an allowed disability. Social Security provides a minimum level of disability protection, however the payments are relatively low and qualifying is quite difficult. Employers may offer group disability income insurance, in which employees are covered under a large plan in which medical exams and specific applications are not required. These group plans may not offer the specific benefits that physicians require (e.g. higher salary coverage, own occupation definition, etc.). An individual disability income insurance plan may be obtained by an individual physician after application through an insurance agent. A medical exam and lab work-up will likely be required. Any pre-existing health conditions (such as a chronic illness, recent surgery, the use of anti-depressant medication, tobacco use, etc.) will raise the premium and lower the benefit offered by the insurance company. Therefore, it is best to apply for disability income insurance before one develops any health problems in order to lock in the maximal benefit at the lowest cost through a plan that is guaranteed renewable. One should also make sure that the ability to increase salary coverage is addressed through a future benefits increase option. Of additional importance to a physician is a policy that covers one's own occupation, or "own-occ." For example, a surgeon who is injured and not able to operate would receive insurance payments even if able to function in a non-surgical capacity. Disability income insurance is expensive; one way to lower costs is to select a longer elimination period, the period of time between when a person becomes disabled and when insurance benefits begin. See also *own occupation* and *elimination period.*

- **Disbursement:** paying or discharging money; the disbursement of a student loan is the transfer of money from the loan company to your school.

- **Diversification:** with investing, one should aim to maximize return while minimizing risk. By spreading out one's investments over different securities that carry different risk attributes and that are *not* correlated, one minimizes unsystematic risk. For example, one may invest in large-cap U.S. stocks, international stocks, U.S. bonds, and REITs. By not having one's money in a single asset one reduces the risk of losing a substantial amount of capital as the result of a single market fluctuation. Further, one is able to take advantage of potential gains in a particular well-performing security that may offset losses from another under-performing security. The end result is decreased portfolio volatility for an equivalent (if not potentially higher) investment return. See *Modern Portfolio Theory.*

- **Dividend:** payment of a portion of a company's profit to shareholders. A stock that sells for $100 and pays $5 has a 5% dividend. Dividends are generally paid on a monthly, quarterly, semi-annual, or annual basis. By reinvesting dividends a young investor can greatly increase portfolio return over time. An older investor in retirement may use dividends as a form of cash-flow (i.e. income).

- **Dollar cost averaging:** the optimal way to purchase securities is to buy low and sell high. Unfortunately, an investor is not able to accurately predict future security prices. By contributing a fixed amount of money into an investment account at regular intervals, the investor is able to accumulate shares at a lower average price-per-share than the simple average of all prices paid. For example, if one contributes $300 per month into an IRA account, the total number of shares purchased will depend on the price-per-share at the time of purchase. When shares are $9/share, the investor will acquire 33.333 shares. When shares are $11/share, the investor will acquire 27.273 shares. Thus, the investor has effectively bought *more* shares at a lower price and *less* shares at a higher price. The average price for the investor's 60.61 shares is $9.90/share (i.e. the weighted average), *not* $10.00/share (the simple average of the two prices paid). Thus, over the long-term, the investor accumulates more shares at a lower per-share cost. Dollar cost averaging has been refuted in the sense that if one has a lump sum of money it is best to invest it all as early as possible in order to maximize time invested in the market; but for the resident-investor, regular monthly contributions do take advantage of dollar cost averaging through the acquisition of more shares at a lower per-share costs over time in the manner described above.

- **Dow Jones Industrial Average:** a price-weighted index of 30 blue-chip stocks traded in the U.S. stock market. It represents mostly industrial companies (such as General Electric). The Dow provides a quick view of how the largest companies in the United States are performing.

- **Down payment:** an amount of money used to secure a loan through the reduction of principal and achievement of equity at the loan's outset. Traditionally, a 20% down payment has been recommended for the purchase of a house. The down payment may be reduced in exchange for a higher interest rate and the addition of private mortgage insurance. A down payment for a house can *not* be made with funds from another loan, i.e. a down payment must be cash only.

- **EAFE:** a stock index that tracks the stock markets of Europe, Australasia, and the Far East (such as China and Japan).

- **Efficient Market Theory:** holds that security prices are priced appropriately automatically and that an investor can not identify a "bargain." The Efficient Market Hypothesis is further broken down into three gradations: weak—market prices already accurately reflect all relevant historical data; semistrong—market prices reflect all historical data and all publicly available information; strong—market prices reflect all historical, current public, and current non-public (i.e. "insider") information. The end result is that an investor can not hope to "beat" the market through technical analysis in the hopes of identifying improperly priced securities, since a security's price *already* reflects all available information. From this, one can deduce that the best an investor can do is to follow the market as a whole and aim to achieve the market's return (for example through low-cost broad-index investing).

- **Elimination period:** in reference to disability income insurance, the elimination period refers to the amount of time that must pass between becoming disabled and the point at which the insurance policy will begin to provide a benefit. For example, if one has a disability income insurance policy with a six-month elimination period and becomes disabled on June 21st, the policy would begin providing a benefit on December 21st. Longer elimination periods lead to lowered premiums.

- **Emerging markets:** the financial markets of developing countries, such as China, India, and the countries of Latin America, Eastern Europe, and Africa.

- **Equifax:** one of the three consumer reporting agencies.

- **Equity:** ownership in a firm, e.g. a stock. May also refer to the dollar difference between what a property could be sold for minus debt owed. The owner of a house that could sell for $300,000 but that has $200,000 owed against it has equity of $100,000.

- **Escrow:** holding of money by a third party until the obligations of a contract are met. For example, the security deposit paid to lease an apartment is held in escrow (i.e. neither in the possession of the landlord nor the tenant). When the lease is concluded the security deposit is returned to the tenant (along with any earned interest) provided that the tenant paid rent and did not inflict excess damage to the property. If the tenant did not comply with the terms of the lease (e.g. there is damage to the property), the landlord may use the money in escrow to cover the associated costs.

- **Expense ratio:** the percentage of assets that an investor in a mutual fund is charged for the maintenance of the mutual fund. It includes management and advisory fees as well as 12b-1 fees. One should always strive to invest in funds with the lowest expenses possible, since this is a known way to increase return over the long-term. A popular way to minimize expense is to invest in low-cost no-load index mutual funds.

- **Experian:** one of the three major consumer reporting agencies.

- **Extended repayment:** in reference to consolidated student loans, an extended repayment schedule may be elected in order to minimize the cost of monthly payments. This of course extends to the total cost paid back over time (for example, over 30 years). If one's consolidation loan has a very low interest rate it may be advantageous to extend the repayment of that loan in order to free up capital for better uses, such as eliminating consumer debt (e.g. credit card debt) and contributing to one's retirement investment accounts.

- **Fair Credit Reporting Act:** addresses the Consumer Reporting Agencies (CRAs). The Fair Credit Reporting Act requires that CRAs enable consumers to access their own credit reports, which includes the distribution of one free credit report (from each of the three major CRAs) per year, available through *www.annualcreditreport.com*. Also stipulated is the necessity for the CRAs to actively work with the consumer to correct identified errors in the credit report. If an error is removed, the CRA must notify the consumer at least 5 days before the removed item is to be re-listed in the credit report. Additionally, CRAs may not keep negative information about a consumer for an extended period of time. For most negative events (such as a late payment) the limit is 7 years; bankruptcy has a limit of 10 years.

- **Federal student loan consolidation:** enables students to consolidate federal student loans (such as Stafford, PLUS, and Perkins loans) into a single large loan with a fixed interest rate and a longer repayment period (which translates into lower monthly payments). A federal student loan consolidation retains the benefits of certain federal loans, such as the payment of interest on subsidized Stafford loans during deferment and the forgiveness of the loan upon the borrower's death.

- **Federal Reserve System:** also referred to as "the Fed." This is the federal banking system of the United States. Created in 1913 and overseen in Washington D.C. by the Federal Reserve Board, it is responsible for directing United States Monetary Policy. One of its relevant functions to investors is the setting of the discount rate on overnight loans of federal funds to banks. It is this discount rate that banks then use to set the "prime rate," which is the interest rate on loans that banks charge to their best customers (generally 3% above the discount rate). In this way, the Fed affects the interest rates charged on bank loans, which in turn affects inflation. Thus, the Fed controls the supply and flow of money within the country. Lower interest rates stimulate the economy by making it easier for individuals and businesses to borrow money (which may increase inflation); higher interest rates slow the economy by increasing the cost of borrowing (which may lower inflation via unemployment, declining production, and ensuing price decreases).

- **Fee-for-service insurance:** also known as "indemnity insurance," a now archaic health-insurance model in which a consumer obtained care from a physician for a specified fee, which was either paid by the consumer out of pocket and then submitted to the insurance company for reimbursement, or submitted by the health care provider's office directly to the insurance company for reimbursement. Such a plan had great freedom (i.e. no limitations on who a patient could obtain care from; no need for referrals to see a specialist, etc.) but required higher out of pocket expenses from the patient. Some feel that fee-for-service insurance contributed to rising health care costs since payment for services did not occur at a discounted rate, nor was there a limiting overseer (such as a primary care physician required to give referrals to see a specialist).

- **FICA:** Federal Insurance Contributions Act; payroll tax that pays for Social Security (retirement and disability benefits) and Medicare.

- **FICO:** Fair Isaac Corporation, the company that has created and implemented the most widely used model for determining a person's credit score. Elements included in the calculation of a FICO credit score include timeliness of payments, the ratio of current revolving debt to the total amount of available credit, length of credit history, types of credit used, and recent attempts at obtaining more credit. One should always pay bills on time, minimize the debt-to-credit ratio, and limit credit inquiries (for example, not applying for store credit cards, etc.).

- **Financial planner:** professional who assists clients with both long and short term financial goals. May make recommendations regarding investments, insurance, and taxes. Fees can be charged either through commission on the sale of products (such as mutual funds), on an hourly rate, or as a percentage of all held assets (such as 1.25% annually from money handled for that year).

- **Fiscal year:** a 12-month period used for calculating annual financial statements in business. It need not begin on January 1. A fiscal quarter is a 3-month period. In the United States, the fiscal year begins on October 1 and ends on September 30 of the following year. Fiscal quarters include the 1st Quarter (October 30 through December 31); 2nd Quarter (January 1 through March 31); 3rd Quarter (April 1 through June 30); 4th Quarter (July 1 through September 30).

- **Fixed-rate mortgage:** the interest rate is predetermined and does not change over the course of the mortgage. This affords predictable monthly payments and predictable loan-life costs.

- **Floor:** in finance, a floor refers to a lower limit; for example, an adjustable rate mortgage may have a floor that limits how low the interest rate may go, regardless of how low the interest rate index drops. No-floor ARMs are better deals than ARMs that have a floor.

- **Forbearance:** a manner of postponing student loan payments. While loans are in forbearance, subsidized loans do *not* have their interest paid by the federal government; therefore, when postponing student loan payments one should try to obtain deferment as opposed to forbearance.

- **Foreclosure:** when a person defaults on a mortgage the bank may elect to seize the property and sell it (i.e. foreclosure) in order to recoup money to pay off the owed debt.

- **Front-end load:** the fee paid by an investor at the time of purchase, for example at the initial purchase of a mutual fund. Since fees reduce return, residents should only purchase no-load mutual funds.

- **Fund management:** a mutual fund is overseen by a fund manager. The fund may be passively managed (for example, an index mutual fund that aims to follow a given index) or actively managed (for example an "aggressive growth fund," which involves active research, trading, etc. in order to purchase stocks for the fund that serve to meet the fund's specific investment strategy, with the ultimate goal being to beat the market as a whole). Active fund management through history has tended to *underperform* passively managed funds. The main reason for this seems to be that actively managed funds inherently are associated with increased fund costs (trading fees, management fees, research fees, capital gains taxes, etc.). Many believe that, given the high improbability of selecting undervalued stocks in an efficient market, the chances of actually beating the market as a whole are extremely low. When additional fees are added, the chance of an actively managed fund beating the market consistently (i.e. over the long term) is almost zero. Therefore, residents are advised to invest in low-cost index mutual funds, which should mirror the market as a whole and thus generate the best return achievable from the market as a whole.

- **Gap insurance:** when one leases an automobile, there is a period of time early on in the lease when the market value of the automobile is notably less than the residual balance of the lease. If the automobile was to be stolen or seriously damaged in a car crash, the standard automobile insurance benefit would be insufficient to pay off the residual lease balance. Gap insurance fills in the "gap" between market value and lease residual value.

- **Grace period:** the period during which no interest is charged on a debt. For student loans, the standard grace period lasts for six months upon leaving school; for credit cards, a grace period may be as short as 21 days.

- **Gross income:** the amount of money earned prior to deductions / payment of taxes.

- **Group insurance:** many employers offer various group insurance policies to their employees, such as health insurance, group term life insurance, and group disability income insurance. Because risk is spread out over the "group," premiums can be effectively lowered when insurance is purchased through a group plan. Such policies also generally do not require specific medical examinations, etc. One must be careful, though, since the level of coverage is often inferior to that obtained through an individual policy. For example, a group term life insurance policy may only provide a death benefit equal to the insured's annual salary. Thus, a person earning $40,000 per year would leave $40,000 to the beneficiary in the event of the insured's death. For someone with children and a mortgage, a death benefit of $500,000 would be more appropriate; therefore, group insurance plans are often not sufficient in and of themselves to adequately insure an individual.

- **Growth stock:** equity in a company that reinvests its earnings in itself in order to grow the company; investors see these companies' shares as having a high potential to generate capital gains.

- **Guaranteed renewable:** a type of insurance policy in which the insurer is required to renew the insurance policy of the insured as long as the insured has made payments according to the agreed upon terms; that is, the insurance policy may not be cancelled as a result of changes in the insured's health status, etc.

- **Guaranteed replacement cost:** an insurance policy that allows for the full replacement of an item at the required cost of replacement, i.e. the policy is not limited to a depreciated valuation of the insured item but instead the policy covers the cost required to replace the item in today's dollars.

- **Hedge:** basically an investment made with the goal of reducing overall portfolio loss should another investment perform poorly.

- **Hedge fund:** a type of mutual fund that is open only to accredited investors (for example, someone with a minimum net worth of at least $1 million); the fund is not regulated by the Securities and Exchange Commission

(SEC) and generally has an extremely high minimum investment. The manager of a hedge fund is usually paid a percentage of profits, termed a *performance fee*. Many hedge funds are based offshore (i.e. outside the U.S.) in order to take advantage of preferable tax climates. Hedge funds can be extraordinarily risky, but they also have the potential to generate astonishing returns.

- **HIPAA:** Health Insurance Portability and Accountability Act of 1996; intended to protect health insurance coverage for workers and their families when they change or lose their jobs; requires the establishment of national standards for electronic health care transactions and, specifically, for maintaining the security and privacy of health data in an effort to encourage the use of electronic health data interchanges. HIPAA also prevents the denial of coverage or the imposition of preexisting condition exclusions on individuals who have had at least 18 months of prior health insurance coverage without any significant breaks in coverage.

- **HMO:** Health Management Organization; a form of managed care in which patients within the HMO are treated by physicians who are members of the HMO; services are delivered at a discounted rate. One limitation of HMOs is the inability for patients to see specialists without first receiving a referral to that specialist from their primary care doctor.

- **Homeowner's insurance:** policy to protect a homeowner's physical property (i.e. the house and personal belongings) as well as to provide liability coverage (in the event that someone sustains an injury on the insured's property).

- **Hybrid ARM:** a mortgage that has a fixed interest rate for one period of time and an adjustable interest rate for another period of time. For example, a mortgage might start off as a fixed-rate mortgage for a period of three years and then "reset" to an adjustable rate mortgage with yearly interest adjustments thereafter. Because some of the risk of interest rate uncertainty is shifted to the borrower, the lender in turn is able to offer a lower initial interest rate.

- **Hybrid automobile:** Today, the vast majority of automobiles on the road use internal combustion engines that burn gasoline or diesel fuel to provide power. The burning of fossil fuels releases carbon into the atmosphere that contributes to global warming. In an effort to reduce the use of fossil fuels, hybrid automobiles have become mainstream. A hybrid automobile has two sources of power: an internal combustion engine that is fueled by gasoline, and an electric motor that is powered by on-board batteries. The motor converts to a generator when the car is decelerating or braking, thus recharging the batteries. By using the electric motor to help propel the car, a hybrid automobile is able to rely less on the internal combustion engine and, at times, even turn the gasoline engine completely off (for example at a stop light). As a result, fuel economy is improved. The most popular hybrid vehicle today, the Toyota Prius, is capable of almost 60 miles-per-gallon during city driving.

- **Income stock:** a stock that has high dividend yields while having a lowered chance for making capital gains. An income fund seeks to invest in such stocks so that the investor sees a real current income as a result of dividend disbursements.

- **Indemnity insurance:** see *fee-for-service*

- **Independent Practice Association (IPA):** a group of physicians who contract together with each other. In turn, this association contracts with an HMO. Physicians practice out of their own offices and are allowed to see both HMO and non-HMO patients (i.e. an open system).

- **Index mutual fund:** a fund that aims to match the returns of a given stock index, such as the Standard & Poor's 500. As a result of matching an index, an index fund is able to operate at lower costs (for example, there is not an expensive research team to pay for, etc.). As a result of lower costs and being invested in a manner that follows the market, index mutual funds have the ability to generate greater returns over the long-term than the majority of actively managed funds (which invariably have higher fees). Index mutual funds should be the foundation of a resident's investment strategy. See also *efficient market theory* and *life-cycle mutual fund*

- **Inflation:** the rate at which the general price for goods and services increases. Since the year 2000 the annual inflation rate has been approximately 3%.

- **Interest capitalization:** when interest accrues on a debt and payments made on that debt are insufficient to cover the accrued interest, the added interest becomes *capitalized*, i.e. it is added to the principal balance. From then on, interest calculations are based on the new principal balance (which is the original balance *plus* the capitalized interest). In this way, the loan debt can increase very rapidly. Thus, residents are advised to at least make interest payments on student loan debts that are in forbearance (or unsubsidized loans in deferment).

- **Internal Revenue Service (IRS):** the federal agency that is in charge of collecting federal income taxes.

- **Investment:** when capital is *invested* it is placed into a vehicle that is believed to generate an increase of that capital over the long term.

- **Investment sector:** refers to a part of the whole; in other words, with investing, capital may be invested in various sectors such as manufacturing, technology, health care, services, etc.

- **Investment vehicle:** Any type of item in which capital is invested is an investment vehicle. For example, stocks, bonds, and mutual funds are all different types of investment vehicles.

- **IRA:** individual retirement account; an IRA may be opened by any employed individual. Contributions may be tax deductible and taxed upon withdrawal (traditional IRA) or may be made with after-tax dollars in order to escape income taxation upon withdrawal (Roth IRA). Gains within the account are tax-deferred, which greatly increases the ability of the invested capital to gain value. There are various restrictions on income in terms of who may claim traditional IRA contributions as tax deductible, and on who may contribute to a Roth IRA. There also is an annual contribution limit, which for 2007 is $4,000 for those under age 50. Traditional IRAs have limitations on the withdrawal of funds (for example a 10% penalty may will be accessed for non-permitted withdrawals) similar to those imposed by a 401(k). On the other hand, Roth IRAs do not have restrictions on the withdrawal of funds.

- **Itemized deductions:** specific deductions permitted by the IRS that reduce one's adjusted gross income. Examples include certain medical expenses and mortgage interest payments.

- **Large cap:** in reference to a stock's market capitalization (the product of the total number of shares outstanding multiplied by the share's price), large-cap refers to the largest U.S. companies, generally with market capitalization greater than ~$10 billion.

- **Level term life insurance:** also referred to as *guaranteed level term life insurance*, this is a life insurance policy in which the premiums and benefits remain constant throughout the term of the policy (e.g. 20 years). This is the recommended form of life insurance for residents.

- **Liability:** in reference to insurance, liability coverage offers protection in the event of personal liability as a result of an individual suffering damages or an injury while on your property or within your automobile. It also covers damage that the policyholder may cause to another person's property. See also *umbrella policy.*

- **Lien:** an asset of a borrower that a lender holds as a form of security for a debt. For example, a lien may be consensual in which the borrower and lender both agree to a lien, such as an automobile for a car loan or a house for a mortgage. A non-consensual lien, in which the borrower has not consented, may be imposed in various settings; for example, a tax lien may be imposed on a property for unpaid property taxes. Tax liens remain with a given property, not with the prior owner; thus, the purchaser of a piece of property with a lien becomes responsible for the past taxes. One must make sure that property (e.g. real estate, automobiles, etc.) does not have a lien when preparing to make a purchase.

- **Life-cycle mutual fund:** a form of asset-allocation mutual fund that automatically diversifies the investor's portfolio among stocks and bonds, as well as among different investment sectors. For example, a life-cycle fund may invest in 90% stocks (through index mutual funds) and 10% bonds (through index bond funds). The stock mutual funds might be further split among the United States, Europe, and emerging markets, etc. Early in the investor's life the fund is invested heavily in stocks (e.g. 90%). As the investor nears retirement, the fund automatically shifts from being heavily invested in stocks towards being more heavily invested in bonds in order to limit short-term volatility and provide consistent investment income.

- **Loan forgiveness:** with federal student loans, debt is forgiven upon the death of the borrower. This prevents the borrower's surviving family (such as a spouse) from having to assume payments on the outstanding educational debt. For private student loans, forgiveness of the debt upon the borrower's death is a feature that is not always a part of the loan agreement; check the promissory notes of your private student loans to see whether loan forgiveness is a part of the loan agreement.

- **Lock-in agreement:** when obtaining pre-approval for a mortgage make sure to get a lock-in agreement, which holds the interest rate over the time-period between the pre-approval and the purchase of a house. Without a lock-in agreement, it is possible for the terms to become less favorable if interest rates have risen during the intervening time period.

- **Marginal tax rate:** to understand the marginal tax rate, first consider that tax brackets range from 10% to 35%. Most residents will fall into the 25% tax bracket, which includes incomes within the range $31,850 to $64,250. Falling within this tax bracket does not mean that you owe 25% of your income. Actually, the tax is assessed at the appropriate percentage incrementally, starting from zero dollars and working up to your final annual income. In other words, if you make $40,000 per year your tax bill is *not* $10,000—it is actually $6,424.25. This figure is arrived at by taxing the first $7,825 (the upper limit for the first tax bracket) of your income at the 10% rate. Your next dollars earned, up to $31,850 (the upper limit for the second tax bracket), are taxed at 15%. Finally, your remaining earned dollars above $31,850 are taxed at your tax bracket rate of 25%. If you earned enough to move into the next tax bracket, your dollars earned beyond $64,250 (the upper limit of the 25% tax bracket) would be taxed at 28%, and so on—up to the 35% tax bracket for those with annual incomes beyond $350,000. Tax bracket specifics can be found at www.irs.gov. The percentage described by your tax bracket is referred to as your *marginal tax rate*. When calculating tax savings (e.g. what are your tax savings when contributing to your 401(k) plan) you should always use the marginal rate, since your savings come off the top of your earnings. Thus, a $1000 contribution to your 401(k) sees a 25% tax savings—it's as if the contribution only cost $750 in out-of-pocket terms (excluding state taxes). The same holds true when predicting the amount of tax you will owe on additional income. For example, if you moonlight and are paid directly without any taxes withheld, you can use your marginal tax rate to predict tax owed. Therefore, a $1000 moonlighting shift really is only going to net you $750 after federal income tax is accounted for.

- **Market capitalization:** a manner of assessing a company's total market value; the figure is arrived at by multiplying the stock price by the total number of shares outstanding (i.e. the number of shares that people own). Large cap stocks are from companies that have values greater than $10 billion, such as blue chips. Mid cap companies have values between $1 billion to $10 billion. Moving down, small caps are valued between $250 million to $1 billion, and micro caps are valued less than $250 million.

- **Medicare:** signed into law by President Lyndon B. Johnson on July 30, 1965, as an amendment to the Social Security legislation. Medicare assists in the payment of hospitalizations and nursing home services (Part A), office visits and durable medical equipment (Part B), and now prescription drugs (Part D) after the signing of the Medicare Prescription Drug, Improvement, and Modernization Act, which was signed into law by President George W. Bush in 2003.

- **Micro-cap:** a company with a market capitalization of less than $250 million. These stocks in general exhibit the highest volatility / risk.

- **Mid-cap:** a company with a market capitalization of between $1 billion to $10 billion.

- **Modern Portfolio Theory:** the theory that rational investors (i.e. investors who are risk-averse), if given the choice between investing in two portfolios with equal returns but different risk attributes, will always choose to invest in the portfolio with less risk (as measured by the standard deviation of the portfolio's valuation). Further, increased risk will only be assumed if it accompanies increased predicted return. Using complicated mathematics, an "efficient frontier" can be identified, which is the degree of diversification that produces the optimal balance of return versus risk. Through diversification, risk can be lowered to this optimal point by holding various investment vehicles that are not perfectly correlated. While a useful concept, it is imperfect since it necessarily relies on historical data to predict future outcomes.

- **Money factor:** a manner of referring to the effective interest rate charged for an automobile lease; but be careful! The money factor itself is not exactly an annual interest rate, but rather a number that just appears to be an interest rate. A money factor may be quoted as 3.0 in an effort to confuse you into thinking it's a 3.0% interest rate. It's not. The 3.0 money factor actually means 0.0030. To calculate your interest rate, multiple the money factor by 2400 (a conversion-constant). In this case, *what you thought was 3.0% interest is actually 7.2%!*

- **Money market account:** a market for the borrowing and lending of money for periods of less than three years; the securities used include U.S. government bonds, T-bills, and commercial paper from banks and companies. A money market fund invests in these short-term securities. Money market funds used to be the preferred savings vehicle, since interest rates could approach 5% (as opposed to typical bank savings account interest rates of <1%). However, with the advent of internet savings accounts (some of which offer interest rates ~5%), money market accounts are being usurped from the preferred savings vehicle position since money markets accounts are not FDIC insured and online bank savings accounts are.

- **Mutual fund:** comprised of pooled investors' money, a mutual fund is able to buy shares in multiple companies, enabling an investor to achieve diversification in a manner that is more efficient and affordable than if the investor had to buy these shares individually. For example, a share of an S&P 500 mutual fund may sell for approximately $100.00—for this investment, the shareholder gets diversification across the entire S&P 500 index. The individual investor would have to spend much more than $100.00 in order to purchase shares of each of the companies listed in the S&P 500 index separately. As a result, mutual funds form the foundation of the majority of individual investors' portfolios. To increase long term returns, no-load low-cost index mutual funds are recommended.

- **NASDAQ:** National Association of Securities Dealers Automatic Quotation system; the NASDAQ is an electronic-screen-based securities exchange. It is based in Times Square, New York City, NY. It is the largest stock exchange in the United States. The NASDAQ trades mostly technology-related stocks.

- **Negative amortization:** a loan repayment schedule in which the principal loan balance actually *increases* over time because the scheduled payments are not sufficient to cover the cost of accrued interest. Accrued interest is then capitalized to the loan's principal balance. Negative amortization can occur when an adjustable rate mortgage resets to a higher interest rate *without* an appropriate adjustment of the monthly payment. Therefore, to avoid negative amortization, one should always ensure that monthly payments adjust accordingly to an interest rate change.

- **Nest egg:** a colloquialism for one's retirement savings

- **Net income:** total income after associated costs are deducted from gross income (such as taxes, fees, etc.).

- **New York Stock Exchange:** (NYSE): Based on Wall Street in New York City, NY, the NYSE is the largest stock exchange in terms of dollar values, and second in size in terms of number of shares traded. The NYSE involves trading through an auction-style format that occurs on the stock exchange floor, where traders are seen yelling and communicating via hand signals. As of January 2007, a portion of the NYSE can now be traded via an electronic interface.

- **No-fault automobile insurance:** Certain states, in an effort to reduce the costs of legal action associated with car crashes, have instituted a "no-fault" automobile insurance policy. Unlike typical automobile insurance (in which fault for causing a car crash must be assigned in order to have the at-fault person's insurance pay for damages), a no-fault policy does not require the determination of fault for a car crash. Rather, each person's automobile insurance covers the damages of each person's own vehicle, as well as potential liability expenses (such as medical care, etc.). Proceeding to lawsuit is forbidden unless a person sustains a particularly severe injury.

- **No-load mutual fund:** a mutual fund in which there is no fee other than the expense ratio of the fund. No-load funds have the potential to yield the best returns over the long-term because the return is not degraded by excess fees. When investing in mutual funds, residents should only deal with no-load mutual funds.

- **Non-cancelable life insurance:** the statute that an insurance policy may not be cancelled by the insurer as long as premiums are paid by the insured, regardless of changes to health condition or risk attributes. May also be referred to as guaranteed renewable. Residents should buy insurance that is non-cancelable / guaranteed renewable.

- **Octane:** an alkane present in gasoline that affects gasoline's resistance to early combustion (i.e. combustion prior to the appropriate time in the engine cycle), which causes engine "knock," a potentially damaging event to an internal combustion engine. High powered engines with high compression ratios are prone to engine knock, and therefore require high octane fuel (i.e. premium gasoline). Smaller engines, with lower compression ratios, are not prone to engine knock and therefore do not require high octane fuel (and will operate perfectly well with regular gasoline). The correct octane fuel to use is the one recommended by the operator's manual of a vehicle. Using premium fuel in a car that only requires regular fuel (i.e. 87 octane) is unnecessary.

- **Open-end lease:** in reference to an automobile lease, the less common open-end lease involves the residual value of the vehicle being recalculated at the time of lease end. If the residual value is less than what was predicted at the beginning of the lease term, the consumer will be liable to pay the difference. A closed-end lease avoids this situation. See *closed-end lease.*

- **Option ARM:** an adjustable rate mortgage that enables the borrower to either make a specified minimum payment, an interest-only payment, or a payment according to the terms of a 15-year or 30-year mortgage. If the payment selected happens to be less than the interest payment, negative amortization will result. Such a mortgage is most appropriate for someone with a sporadic and irregular income, therefore an option ARM is not the best choice for a resident.

- **Own-occupation:** when setting up disability income insurance, it is important for a physician to obtain a policy that covers one's "own occupation." In other words, someone who becomes unable to perform the duties of one's specific specialty would still receive benefits regardless of whether one is still able to perform some other duties. Consider, for example, a surgeon who is injured and becomes unable to operate. If this surgeon had a standard disability income insurance plan and was still able to perform *some* kind of work (such as non-operative duties) the plan would not pay anything, even if the new salary earned by the surgeon was much less than what was previously earned while operating. On the other hand, if the surgeon had a policy with an own-occupation definition, the surgeon would receive insurance payments even while working in this other capacity. Often, the amount paid in this case is reduced in relation to how much the person is able to earn; of course, this is better than nothing, which would be the situation without the own-occupation policy. Own-occupation is sometimes referred to as "own-occ."

- **Participant-directed 401(k):** type of 401(k) retirement account in which the individual employee chooses how to invest the account's money; for example, one may choose which mutual funds to buy, etc.

- **Pay yourself first:** the single most important concept in saving for one's future; the first bill that is paid should be a payment to oneself. That is, even before paying rent, a certain amount of money from each paycheck (such as 10%) should be contributed to a retirement account (such as a 401(k)/403(b)/457 or IRA). Ideally, this should be accomplished automatically either through your employer's payroll office (in the case of a 401(k), 403(b), or 457) or by setting up automatic contributions online through the brokerage company handling your IRA. Contributing regularly also allows you to take advantage of dollar cost averaging. See *dollar cost averaging.*

- **Permanent life insurance:** life insurance vehicles that build a cash-value over time (unlike term life insurance, which does not build a cash value). As a result of building cash value there is an associated increase in cost to the purchaser. The ability of the policy to build a cash value can be useful to an older person as concerns with taxes and leaving an estate to heirs presents itself, however younger people (such as residents) are likely better off purchasing the much more affordable term-life insurance.

- **Personal injury protection (PIP):** an extension of automobile insurance; PIP pays for medical damages, lost wages, and other potential damages in the event of a car crash. It is generally not necessary if one has good health insurance coverage, since PIP would only begin coverage after one's health insurance benefits had been exhausted. PIP is required, however, in states that institute a no-fault automobile insurance model.

- **PMI:** Private Mortgage Insurance: Required by lenders when the borrower's equity (or down payment) is less than 20% of the purchase price of the house. The cost is usually a certain percentage (such as 0.5%) of the total borrowed amount. PMI is intended to protect the lender (via repayment of the mortgage) in the event that the borrower defaults on the mortgage. The cost of PMI can be paid up front, or it may be capitalized into the total loan balance. Some recommend taking the latter approach if one plans to be in the home for a relatively short period of time since, during the early years of mortgage repayment, payments are mostly towards interest, which is deductible from one's federal income taxes.

- **Points:** in reference to a mortgage, a point represents 1% of the loan amount. Points may be paid up front in order to lower the loan's interest rate. General recommendations are to avoid paying points if one plans to remain in a house for a shorter period of time. The reasoning is that paid mortgage interest is tax-deductible. Since during the first few years of paying a mortgage most repayment is towards interest (and is therefore recouped as a tax-deduction), it does not make sense to pay money up front and out of pocket in order to lower the interest rate.

- **Portfolio:** a general term referring to a collection of investments.

- **Portfolio rebalancing:** assuming one has devised an asset allocation scheme, the relative proportion of investments would change over time as each investment gains or loses value. For example, a portfolio beginning with 80% stocks and 20% bonds may, over the course of a year, shift to 90% stocks and 10% bonds as a result of changing stock and bond values. In order to return to the original asset allocation plan, the investor must sell investments that have become over-represented in the portfolio and buy investments that have become under-represented in the portfolio. Thus, in the above example, one would sell stocks and purchase bonds so that the balance is brought to 80% stocks and 20% bonds. The purpose of all of this is to maintain diversification within the portfolio in order to maximize risk-adjusted return.

- **POS:** an acronym for "point of service," a type of managed-care health plan in which the patient may select whether to have billing occur as if participating either in an HMO or a PPO; this selection is made at the time of receiving care, i.e. at the point of service.

- **PPO:** an acronym for "preferred provider organization." This is a type of managed care model in which health care providers have contracted with the insurance company to provide care to the company's enrolled population at discounted rates. One of the key differences between HMOs and PPOs is that patients do not require referrals from their primary care provider in order to have access to a specialist within a PPO.

- **Pre-approval:** in the setting of purchasing real estate, it is beneficial for the buyer to have been already reviewed by a lender and determined to be approved for a mortgage up to a certain dollar amount. The key benefit is that a buyer will be able to move quickly with an offer to a seller, which can be particularly beneficial in an active real estate market. Further, the buyer gets a picture of what their mortgage terms will be; this can be valuable in determining how much one ought to spend on a property.

- **Pre-certification:** some managed care plans (such as HMOs) require the prior approval of hospitalizations and surgeries. This is intended to control costs, since presumably procedures and admissions deemed "not medically necessary" would be stopped before having occurred, thus saving the managed care organization, the provider, and the patient the troubles of dealing with payment refusal from the managed care organization after the procedure or admission has already occurred.

- **Pre-payment:** a loan's total cost over the life of the loan can be greatly reduced via pre-payment, which is paying *more* than what is required in terms of a minimum monthly payment. One popular manner of accomplishing pre-payment with a mortgage is to make mortgage payments on a bi-weekly basis, which over the course of a year leads to one full month's extra payment being made towards the loan's principal balance (as long as it is specified that the extra payment should be applied to principal balance and *not* towards future interest). Pre-payment can save money over the long-term, and may be a good idea for someone who plans to live in a house for the long term (e.g. > 10 years), or for someone with significant student debt with a relatively high interest rate (e.g. >6%). On the other hand, someone who plans to live in a house for a short period of time (~5 years) or who has a very low interest rate on their student loans (e.g. <3%) should not pre-pay these loans but should instead direct extra money into eliminating consumer debt (credit cards) and into retirement investment accounts. Nevertheless, the prudent borrower always ensures that loans do *not* charge pre-payment penalty fees.

- **Price/Earnings Ratio:** the price of a stock share may be viewed as a multiple of earnings per stock. For example, a company that has a profit of $1 million and has 1 million shares outstanding has an earning of $1 per stock share per year. If a share of that stock is selling for $15, it has a P/E ratio of 15 (which is the historic average). Another way to view this is: How many dollars per share will investors pay for one dollar of earnings per share from a given company. Companies that are expected to do well and grow might garner a price with a P/E ratio of 20 or more. On the other hand, investors might only be willing to pay 10 times earnings for stock in a company that is seen as less robust. The position of the P/E ratio can be a relative barometer of the stock market's optimism. High P/E = optimistic. Unfortunately, extremely high P/E ratios can not be sustained for excessively long periods of time. For example, if P/E ratios began to approach 80, one might expect that an ensuing decline in stock prices would be fast approaching as the market prepared to reset itself.

- **Prime rate:** generally the interest rate that banks charge on loans to their best customers (i.e. those with the best credit scores). In some cases, customers with excellent credit histories may obtain loans at rates that are even *below* the prime rate.

- **Principal:** the face amount of a debt, i.e. the amount borrowed or lent. It is the balance from which interest accrual is calculated.

- **Private student loan:** a student loan from an authority other than the United States Federal government. These loans are not granted according to financial need. Often, the interest rates and terms are not as preferable as those offered by federal student loans. Unfortunately, as education costs have risen, the amount of funds needed by students often exceeds the limits allowed through federal loan programs—thus, students must turn to private student loans. It is important to work with one's financial aid office in an effort to obtain the best financing. Be aware that many private student loans are not forgiven in the case of the borrower's death, thus one's spouse could become liable for student debt. As always, it is important to attempt to borrow the least amount possible by minimizing rent costs and living frugally—the money not borrowed now will save you money many times over in the course of the repayment of your student loans.

- **Property tax:** a tax levied on real estate, usually as a percentage of the property's assessed value. Property taxes can include school taxes and local government taxes. It is important to account for projected property taxes when contemplating the purchase of a home.

- **Real estate:** a piece of land, including whatever property is on the land.

- **Realtor:** a person who is specially trained and licensed through the National Association of Realtors who aids in the buying and selling of real estate.

- **REIT:** Real Estate Investment Trust: a closed-end mutual fund that invests in real estate and loans secured by real estate; REITs offer a hedge against inflation since real estate values tend to move with inflation.

- **Renter's insurance:** when renting an apartment, renter's insurance offers liability protection (in the event that someone sustains an injury while within your apartment), liability to damage that you may cause to the building structure as a whole (for example if you leave the bath tub filling and it overflows, causing water damage to the floor), and personal property protection (in the event of theft, etc.).

- **Replacement value:** as opposed to *actual cost* coverage (which covers the cost paid for an item), items insured for their *replacement value* will be covered up to the cost of replacing that item. This is especially useful if a home is insured; should the home be lost to fire and the homeowner needs to rebuild, it is very possible that the cost of rebuilding from the ground up could cost more money than what was paid for the house initially. In this case, replacement value would cover the cost of rebuilding.

- **Residency relocation loan:** a private loan that is meant to provide cash flow to a graduating medical student. The terms of such a loan are generally not as good as those found with federal student loans (for example, interest rates may be >9%; although this is still less than the average interest rate for a credit card), but the residency relocation loan provides a good source of money when a graduating medical student may need it most. Because the interest rate is well-above the rate of inflation and federal student loan interest rates, one should prioritize paying off a residency relocation loan as quickly as possible.

- **Residual value:** at the end of an automobile lease, the leased vehicle has a new, depreciated value compared to when the car was new. This is the residual value. The capitalized cost and the estimated residual value are used to calculate the expected depreciation of the automobile over the term of the lease which, together with the money factor, are combined to calculate a monthly lease payment. With an open-end lease, if the actual market value at the end of the lease is less than the calculated residual value the consumer may be liable to pay the difference. This is not the case with a closed-end lease.

- **Reversion to the Mean (RTM):** over the very long term, the stock market has always returned to an average real return (i.e. after-inflation return) of ~7%. There will be periods of exaggerated growth and exaggerated decline, but each of these will likely eventually reset back to the normal historical growth rate. This concept can be taken further to predict that one should not invest in "last years best mutual fund," since RTM predicts that winners can't be winners forever. What goes up must come down, and what goes down must come up (to the nominal market return). This is further support that one is best suited to invest in a broad market index mutual fund.

- **Rider:** any alteration to an insurance policy's standard terms.

- **Rollover:** when one leaves employment with a company that provided a 401(k) or 403(b), the person's retirement savings may be relocated (via a rollover) into an IRA (either one that already is established or into a new IRA opened specifically for these funds).

- **Roth IRA:** named for Republican U.S. Senator from Delaware William Roth, the Roth IRA essentially reverses the model of the traditional IRA. With a Roth IRA, contributions are made with after-tax dollars and all withdrawals upon retirement are *tax-free*. Also, there are fewer restrictions on withdrawing money prior to retirement. Unlike the traditional IRA, which has essentially the same withdrawal restrictions, penalties, and exceptions as a 401(k), the Roth IRA allows you to withdraw money that you've contributed at any time without penalty (since the contributions were made with after-tax dollars and therefore are not assigned a special status). This is another reason for the popularity of Roth IRAs. On the other hand, any gains from contributions may not be withdrawn until after age 59 ½, although there is an exception: up to $10,000 of earnings may be withdrawn in order to acquire a principal residence. Because of its reversal of the traditional IRA model, a Roth IRA is best-suited for someone who anticipates being in a higher tax bracket upon retirement, since the funds are contributed while in the lower tax bracket and then distributed exempt from tax while the person is in the higher tax bracket. For this reason, the Roth IRA is a highly recommended choice for residents who can reasonably assume that their retirement income will be higher than their current income. Unfortunately there are income restrictions that limit who may contribute to a Roth IRA. For 2007, the income limits for being able to contribute to a Roth IRA maximally are $95,000 for a single person and $150,000 for a married couple filing jointly. The maximum amount that may be contributed to a Roth IRA is $4,000 for 2007 for those under age 50.

- **R^2:** R-squared. The square of the correlation coefficient; it is used to indicate the degree of fit. An R-squared of 0 indicates no statistical relationship. An R-squared of 100 indicates perfect correlation. In finance, R-squared is used to indicate the degree of correlation between an equity and a given benchmark, such as the S&P 500.

- **Rule of 72:** a quick and easy formula that can be used to predict the amount of time in which money will double when earning compound interest: simply divide 72 by the interest rate. For example, if the interest rate is 10% the amount of time needed for invested money to double is 7.2 years (72 divided by 10). One can also calculate what interest an investment would need to earn in order to double in value within a certain period of time. For example, if one wanted an investment to double in value in 5 years, that investment would have to earn 14.4% interest (72—divided by—desired number of years to double in value; i.e. 72/5 = 14.4).

- **Russell 2000:** a small-cap index that is composed of the 2000 smallest securities of the Russell 3000 (a broad-market index that covers 98% of the U.S. stock market).

- **S&P 500:** Standard & Poor's 500, an index containing the stocks of 500 large cap corporations. It is the second most commonly referred-to market index after the Dow Jones Industrial Average. The first index mutual fund (created by Vanguard) tracked the S&P 500 index. It still remains one of the most popular investment vehicles today.

- **Schedule C Income:** when filing federal income taxes, money earned through moonlighting that did not have income tax withheld will be reported as "other income" under schedule C. Here it is possible to record deductions such as mileage on your car (if it was used to travel to and from the hospital), meals while on the job, etc. Good recordkeeping (e.g. sales receipts, etc.) is key to validating these deductions in the event of an audit.

- **Scheduled coverage:** whereas a general homeowner's policy insures one's personal property within the home up to a fixed percentage of the policy's face value, some may wish to add scheduled coverage, which specifically insures particular items (such as paintings, jewelry, etc.) The "schedule" indicates the amount of insurance coverage applied to each specific item.

- **Secondary market:** investors buy shares of stock directly from a company during an Initial Public Offering (IPO). After the IPO, the majority of shares trade hands from investor to investor, not from investor to issuing company. This buying and selling of shares between investors occurs in what is termed the *secondary market*. This may also be called the *aftermarket*.

- **Securities:** records (either paper or electronic) indicating ownership of stocks or bonds.

- **Security deposit:** when renting an apartment (or leasing an automobile), a security deposit may be required to serve as collateral for the return of the leased property in good condition. This is often a full month's rent when leasing an apartment, and a variable amount when leasing an automobile. Upon return of the leased property it is important to review the condition of the property with the landlord to ensure that both parties agree on the condition of the apartment. With an automobile, it is wise to obtain a *condition report*, which will detail the condition of the automobile and avoid a hassle later on should the dealership try to collect money for damages to the vehicle. The security deposit should be held in an escrow account (i.e. a third-party account). Interest that may be earned on this money should be returned to the consumer.

- **Share:** a unit of ownership of a stock, mutual fund, or REIT.

- **Sharpe Ratio:** Named after Nobel laureate and Stanford University professor William Forsyth Sharpe, who developed the ratio to indicate an investment's mean excess of return per unit of risk. The calculation involves subtracting the risk-free rate of return (such as from a T-bill) from a portfolio's actual rate of return and dividing this by the standard deviation of the portfolio's return. A higher value indicates a better risk-adjusted return.

- **Small-cap:** short for small market capitalization: refers to a company with a market capitalization of between approximately $250 million to $1 billion. Historically, small-cap stocks have exhibited higher volatility than large-cap stocks; the trade-off for this increased volatility has been higher returns over the long term. Whether this trend will continue in the future is up for debate.

- **Social Security:** to pull the country out of the Great Depression, President Franklin D. Roosevelt established the New Deal. One of the key elements to this plan was Social Security, which was (and still is) federally mandated insurance that would provide some level of benefits in the event of injury-induced disability or congenital disability (e.g. severe mental retardation), unemployment, and retirement. It was signed into law in 1935. Prior to this, there was no real safety-net to help people who became disabled or who were born too ill to ever work. Social security is funded by a payroll tax: 6.2% of the employee's income, matched by another 6.2% from the employer, for a total of 12.4%. It is often listed on a pay-stub as FICA (which may also include Medicare, an additional 2.9% payroll tax). A person is eligible to receive Social Security benefits if he or she (or the person's spouse) has worked and paid Social Security taxes for at least a period of 10 years.

- **Speculation:** whereas an investment involves the purchase of risk-adjusted equities to be held for the long term with the appropriately high expectation of earning a return, a speculation involves the purchase of riskier equities with the expectation that ensuing price changes will lead to sizeable profits.

- **Stafford loans:** government-guaranteed student loans named in honor of the late Senator Robert T. Stafford of Vermont. Stafford loans generally have an interest rate that is lower than privately obtained educational loans. For example, Stafford loans are currently charging approximately 6.8% interest. Interest accrual on a Stafford loan is affected by whether the loan is subsidized or unsubsidized. A subsidized Stafford loan has its interest paid by the government while the student is matriculated and for up to three years of post-graduate training (such as residency). This type of loan is awarded based on financial need. According to studentaid.ed.gov, the maximum amount of subsidized funds available to a medical (i.e. graduate) student is $8,500 per year. Once this limit is reached, money is borrowed from the unsubsidized pot, which allows you to borrow an additional $10,000 per year (for 2007) on top of your subsidized loans. Unsubsidized loans are not awarded according to financial need. The total cumulative Stafford loan debt (subsidized plus unsubsidized) is currently $138,500 for graduate students. For unsubsidized Stafford loans, interest begins accumulating as soon as the loan money is disbursed. As the interest accumulates it will be capitalized (usually every quarter, i.e. three months), which means the interest owed gets added to the principal balance (unless the interest is paid prior to capitalization).

- **Stagflation:** the combination of slow (i.e. stagnant) economic growth with rising prices (i.e. inflation).

- **Standard deduction:** as an alternative to itemizing deductions on one's federal income tax return, the IRS allows people to claim a basic amount of money as the *standard deduction*, i.e. a non-itemized deduction. In 2006 the standard deduction was $5,150 for a single filer and $10,300 for a married couple filing jointly.

- **Stock:** ownership of a portion of a corporation; the units of ownership are termed *shares*.

- **Stock exchange:** a company that provides facilities for traders and stock brokers to buy and sell stocks and other securities.

- **Stock index:** a list of stocks that are categorized together based on some commonality, such as market capitalization, sector, etc. Two of the most popular stock indices are the Dow Jones Industrial and the Standard & Poor's 500. The S&P 500 is a common index on which many mutual funds are based. Often, such indices serve as a benchmark for the performance of the stock market as a whole.

- **Stock market:** a term that conceptually encompasses the market in which equities are bought and sold. The actual buying and selling of these equities occurs through a stock exchange.

- **Student loan consolidation:** the combining of all of one's separate student loans into a single consolidated loan. The interest rate of the new loan is the weighted average of the interest rates of the original student loans. Loan consolidation offers two main benefits: a) simplification through the management of a single loan with a fixed interest rate as opposed to many loans with variable interest rates; b) the ability to extend payments over a much greater length of time (such as 30 years) which allows lower monthly payments at the expense of a higher total loan-cost over the whole course of repayment. If the interest rate on the consolidated loan is low (such as less than inflation, ~3-4%), it makes sense to extend the repayment of the loan over time to achieve lower monthly payments; with the monthly savings, extra money can be used to pay off consumer debt (such as credit cards) and to invest in one's retirement account (e.g. 401(k)/403(b) or IRA). Be aware that a loan consolidation may involve a change of the original loans' terms. For example, Stafford loans offer loan forgiveness upon the borrower's death—this benefit is maintained through a federal loan consolidation. Private consolidation loans may not offer this loan forgiveness; be sure to check the promissory note for details.

- **Subsidized loan:** federal Stafford student loans may be subsidized or unsubsidized. Subsidized loans are preferable because the interest is paid by the federal government while the student is matriculated, during grace period, and during deferment (but not during forbearance). Unsubsidized loans never have the interest paid for by the federal government, and therefore interest begins accruing as soon as the loan monies are disbursed.

- **Substantially equal periodic payments (SEPP):** a method by which, under certain circumstances, money may be withdrawn from retirement accounts (401(k)/403(b)/traditional IRA) prior to age 59 ½ without incurring the 10% early withdrawal penalty fee. There are three methods that may be used for calculating the permitted amount of money that may be withdrawn: a) required minimum distribution method, based on the life expectancy of the account owner using the IRS tables for required minimum distributions; b) fixed amortization method over the life expectancy of the owner; c) fixed annuity method using an annuity factor from a reasonable mortality table

- **Synthetic oil:** a type of motor oil used in a variety of applications (most notably in automobile engines) that is non-petroleum based. It is believed to offer the following advantages over conventional motor oil: a) measurably better low and high temperature viscosity performance: b) better chemical & shear stability; c) decreased evaporative loss; d) resistance to oxidation, thermal breakdown and oil sludge problems; e) extended drain intervals with the environmental benefit of less waste oil disposal.

- **Tax bracket:** Tax brackets are categories of income levels that progressively increase the percentage of your income that you owe in tax. Another way of looking at this is that the tax *bracket* is the percentage of tax that you are charged on the last dollar that you earn during a year. Your tax *rate* is actually lower than your tax bracket (unless you have an income that is less than $7,825 for the year 2007). Tax brackets range from 10% to 35%. Most residents will fall into the 25% tax bracket, which includes incomes within the range $31,850 to $64, 250. Falling within this tax bracket does not mean that you owe 25% of your income. Actually, the tax is assessed at the appropriate percentage incrementally, starting from zero dollars and working up to your final annual income. In other words, if you make $40,000 per year your tax bill is *not* $10,000—it is actually $6,424.25. This figure is arrived at by taxing the first $7,825 (the upper limit for the first tax bracket) of your income at the 10% rate. Your next dollars earned, up to $31,850 (the upper limit for the second tax bracket), are taxed at 15%. Finally, your remaining earned dollars above $31,850 are taxed at your tax bracket rate of 25%. If you earned enough to move into the next tax bracket, your dollars earned beyond $64,250 (the upper limit of the 25% tax bracket) would be taxed at 28%, and so on—up to the 35% tax bracket for those with annual incomes beyond $350,000. The percentage described by your tax bracket is also referred to as your *marginal rate*. When calculating tax savings (e.g. what are your tax savings when contributing to your 401(k) plan) you should always use the marginal rate, since your savings come off the top of your earnings. Thus, a $1000 contribution to your 401(k) sees a 25% tax savings—it's as if the contribution only cost $750 in out-of-pocket terms (excluding state taxes). The same holds true for when predicting the amount of tax you will owe on additional income. For example, if you moonlight and are paid directly without any taxes withheld, you can use your marginal rate to predict tax owed. Therefore, a $1000 moonlighting shift really is only going to net you $750 after federal income tax is accounted for.

- **Tax deduction:** an expense that the IRS allows one to deduct from one's taxable income. Tax deductions effectively lower one's gross income to arrive at one's *adjusted gross income*, from which one's tax liability is calculated.

- **Tax-deferred retirement plan:** includes plans that may be employer-sponsored (such as a 401(k) or 403(b)) or that are owned by an individual (such as an IRA). Contributions may be made on a pre-tax basis (401(k)/403(b)), a tax-credited basis (traditional IRA), or with after-tax dollars (Roth IRA). In all cases, money grows in a tax-free shelter. Funds from either a 401(k)/403(b) or traditional IRA are then subjected to federal income tax upon withdrawal during retirement. Funds from a Roth IRA are not subjected to federal income tax at the time of withdrawal [since contributions to a Roth IRA were made with after-tax (i.e. *already* taxed) dollars].

- **T-Bill:** treasury bill; a short-term (less than one-year maturity) debt obligation issued by the United States Treasury. The bills are issued at a discounted value; the face value is then paid upon maturity of the bill. The difference between the discounted price and the face value is the effective interest-earned from this investment. Many investors consider T-bills to be the closest one can achieve to a risk-free investment. The trade-off for such a low risk is a relatively low rate of return compared to stocks, with T-bills typically returning just under 5%.

- **Teaser rate:** often the first month's interest on an adjustable rate mortgage may be especially low, such as 3%. Because this interest rate only lasts for one year, after which the ARM interest rate resets according to its index, it is sometimes referred to as the *teaser rate*. A low initial interest rate does have as a potential benefit the ability to build equity in a property more quickly, assuming one pays more than interest-only payments.

- **Term:** the specific period of time during which a contract (e.g. loan, insurance policy, etc.) is in force.

- **Term life insurance:** an insurance policy that provides a death benefit in the event of the insured's death; however, unlike permanent life insurance, term life insurance does not build a cash value. For this reason, term life insurance is much more affordable than permanent life insurance. Level term life insurance has a set premium cost over the course of the term (for example, 20 years). During this time, the policy can not be cancelled and the premiums will not increase as long as the insured does not default on payments. Level term life insurance is the correct choice of coverage for residents. If one is single, life insurance is a low priority. If one has a spouse, children, and/or a mortgage, life insurance becomes more important since there are others who would suffer as a result of your lost income.

- **Tire rotation:** the movement of automobile tires from back to front and left to right, the purpose of which is to prevent uneven wear patterns from developing on the tires, thus extending tire life and driving safety. This should be performed according to the recommended schedule in your automobile's service manual.

- **Title:** a formal document that serves as proof of ownership for a property (e.g. automobile, house, etc.)

- **Tort:** a civil wrong (such as negligence) recognized by a civil jurisdiction as grounds for a lawsuit.

- **Tort reform:** a movement to curtail the resultant legal inefficiency and economic drain associated with massive lawsuit settlements and the impetus for filing a lawsuit that such high monetary awards bring. Examples of topics addressed by tort reform include limits on non-economic damages;

product liability reform; punitive damages; medical liability reform; joint and several liability; and class action reform. An example of a case that demonstrates the argument in favor of tort reform is the recent $65 million "pants lawsuit" of *Pearson v. Chung*, which was the case of a family-owned dry cleaning business being sued for $67 million in damages as a result of the plaintiff allegedly receiving the wrong pair of pants. The plaintiff lost and was (appropriately) required to pay the defendant's legal fees.

- **Traditional IRA:** traditional individual retirement account. With a traditional IRA, contributions are made in a tax-deferred manner. Since the IRA is not administered by your employer, the funds can't be taken from your paycheck prior to taxes. You make the contributions yourself. The good part is that these contributions are then deducted from your adjusted gross income. You therefore reduce your taxable income and, thus, reduce your total tax bill. If your salary is $40,000 and you contribute $4,000 to a traditional IRA, your taxable income becomes $36,000 (i.e. 40,000-4,000). The earnings in your traditional IRA grow tax-free. There are no upper income limits that would prevent you from being able to contribute to a traditional IRA, however there are income restrictions that limit to what degree someone may claim traditional IRA contributions as tax deductions. For a single person in 2007, the full contribution is tax deductible up to an annual income of $50,000. Above this, the amount of the contribution that is tax deductible phases out to zero when the annual income reaches $60,000. For a married couple filing jointly in 2007, contributions are fully tax deductible up to a combined annual income of $80,000, phasing out to zero by a combined income of $100,000. Withdrawals may not be made from a traditional IRA until after the age of 59 ½; doing so earlier will incur a 10% early withdrawal fee, in addition to the assessment of any owed federal income tax. Furthermore, withdrawals *must* begin at age 70 ½; failing to initiate withdrawals by this age would result in the assessment of a 50% penalty on expected minimal distributions. The traditional IRA is best for someone who expects to be in a lower tax bracket upon retirement. In other words, someone who is in a 25% tax bracket now can realize immediate tax savings by contributing to a traditional IRA. Then, during retirement, when the person's tax bracket may be lower (e.g. 15%), the withdrawals will be subject to that tax rate (15%), for a savings of 10% over the working-years rate of ~25%. One problem here is that it is impossible to predict what tax rates will be in the future. What we anticipate today as a 15% tax bracket for a retired person could change. In the future, our example retired person might, even with the lower income, be assessed a 25% federal income tax simply because Congress could have increased taxes! So a savings in absolute tax terms is not a guarantee. Because a resident is likely taxed in a lower tax bracket now than what can be expected as a retired physician, the Roth IRA is actually recommended over the traditional IRA.

- **TransUnion:** one of the three major consumer reporting agencies that generate credit reports.

- **Trustee-directed 401(k):** a 401(k) in which investment decisions are made by a board of trustees as opposed to being managed by the employee, as in the *participant-directed 401(k)*.

- **UM/UIM:** uninsured / underinsured motorist coverage. Provides coverage in the event of an at-fault party having inadequate or no automobile insurance. It also provides coverage in the event of a hit-and-run car crash. A good rule-of-thumb is to carry the same amount of UM/UIM coverage as your bodily injury liability coverage, e.g. 100/300.

- **Umbrella liability policy:** separate liability coverage that provides protection above and beyond the liability coverage offered by one's homeowner's and automobile insurance policies. A person with high net wealth and/or a high income would be wise to have an adequate umbrella policy, since a benefit is paid in the event of a lawsuit, etc. A typical policy may be for coverage of $1 million to $2 million in blanket liability coverage.

- **Underwriting:** in reference to insurance, underwriting is the process of assessing the risk of potentially insuring someone or something (i.e. the attempt to predict the likelihood that an insurance policy will actually have to pay out in relation to the calculated risk). Factors taken into consideration include age, use of tobacco, past medical history, occupation, risky activities, etc. The result of the process is the determination of how much coverage to offer and at what price said coverage ought to cost.

- **Unsubsidized loan:** an unsubsidized Stafford student loan does not have its interest paid for by the federal government at any period; interest begins accruing immediately upon disbursement of the loan funds. Accrued interest is usually capitalized on a quarterly basis. To avoid interest capitalization, accrued interest should be paid as it becomes due each quarter.

- **Value averaging:** proposed by Michael Edleson of the Harvard Business School, value averaging is a technique of contributing money into one's investment portfolio at a rate dependent upon the portfolio's accrued value in relation to your expected value. In other words, if you decide that you need

$1 million to retire, and you expect an 8% rate of return in your portfolio, you can calculate how much your portfolio should be worth at any given time. You then track your portfolio's market value in relation to your expected value. If the portfolio is worth less than expected at a certain time-point, you must contribute additional funds to bring it up to your target. If it is above your predicted value, you may reduce your contributions or even sell some investments off to bring the value back down to your target point. The end result is buying low (that is, contributing extra money when the portfolio is at a low point and valued below your target point) and selling high (that is, selling when the portfolio is valued above your target point). This can be an interesting way to keep close track of your investments and to force you into a savings strategy, but, since it relies on pre-determined value points, it doesn't actually increase your total return over the long term, although it will likely lower your cost-basis. See also *dollar cost averaging*.

- **Value stock:** simply a stock with a relatively low price-to-earnings ratio (e.g. below the historical average of about P/E 15). The idea is that stocks with low P/E ratios are "cheap," and therefore have greater potential to rise in value.

- **Vehicle Identification Number (VIN):** like a person's social security number, an automobile's VIN is a unique number that identifies the automobile's make, model, year, country of origin, and accident history. When purchasing a used car, the VIN can be checked through services such as CarFax to verify that the car has not been in a car crash, stolen, or affected by a lien.

- **Volatility:** the risk of an investment as calculated by the standard deviation of that investment's return over time. A more volatile asset tends to have wider swings in valuation over time (i.e. greater gains and greater losses), whereas a less volatile asset tends to have a more stable value over time (smaller gains and smaller losses over time). This does not necessarily predict the long term return of an investment, but rather only the propensity for an investment to have value changes over the short term.

- **W-2 Form:** IRS Wage and Tax Statement. Usually received by an employee in mid to late January. This form lists wages earned and taxes withheld. The information from the W-2 is used to complete one's federal and state income tax returns.

- **W-4 Form:** IRS tax form used to indicate the amount of tax withheld from an employee's pay. Claiming 0 deductions would lead to the maximum amount withheld each pay period. Claiming 1 deduction causes more money to be withheld; claiming 2 deductions leads to even more money withheld, and so on. Ideally, one wants to have just the correct amount of tax withheld so as not to owe income tax in April. If a resident earns a lot of untaxed income through moonlighting, selecting 0 deductions may help to avoid having to pay a hefty tax bill in April.

- **Waiver of premiums:** a desirable feature of disability income insurance that eliminates the need to continue the payment of premiums when the insured is deemed disabled and is collecting benefits. Make sure that your disability income insurance policy includes this.

- **Whole life insurance:** a type of permanent life insurance that has both insurance and investment components. The policy pays a death benefit in the event of the insured's death; it also builds a cash value that the policyholder may redeem or borrow against. Because such a policy tends to be more expensive than term life insurance, it is not recommended for residents who, for life insurance coverage, should purchase level term life insurance and, for investing, should contribute to their retirement investment accounts.

- **Wilshire 5000:** Dow Jones Wilshire 5000 Composite Index; an index that is based on the entire United States stock market (currently ~7000 equities). Whereas the S&P 500 effectively covers approximately 75% of the U.S. stock market, the Wilshire 5000 attempts to cover >99% of the U.S. stock market (that is all equities with readily available prices, including those listed on the NYSE, the NASDAQ, the American Stock Exchange, REITs, etc.).

7199310R0

Made in the USA
Lexington, KY
29 October 2010